Confessions
of a Trauma
Therapist

Confessions of a Trauma Therapist

A MEMOIR OF HEALING

AND TRANSFORMATION

To Rose Ann

Mary K. Armstrong

With best wishes &
thanks for all your
help & friendship

Mary

BPS
books

Published in 2010 by
BPS Books
Toronto and New York
bpsbooks.com
A division of Bastian Publishing Services Ltd.

ISBN 978-1-926645-19-3

Cataloguing-in-Publication Data available from Library and Archives Canada.

Cover design: Gnibel
Text design and typesetting: Casey Hooper Design

To Dr. Ralph Bierman,
psychologist and grand old man of
Experiential Psychotherapy
who died in October 2008,
before this book could be published.

Your wisdom, warmth, and compassion
guided me in my healing and in writing this book.
I miss you, Ralph.

Contents

PART III / Finding Lost Memories, Finding Myself

Preface

I can't believe my life turned out so well. As I write this I am sitting in the sunshine on the spacious deck of the cottage my husband, Harvey, and I built when we were young. Our son, Frank, was two years old when we bought this island property on Georgian Bay. That was in 1971. Harvey was about to write his final exams in child and adolescent psychiatry at the University of Toronto. I was a yoga teacher, in the days before yoga was popular. Immersing myself in this ancient discipline was bringing me a deep sense of peace and fulfillment. I was growing and maturing in a guru–disciple relationship with my spiritual teacher, Swami Sivananda Radha. She and I had a close personal relationship, one I look back on now as a ten-year apprenticeship in Eastern philosophy and psychology.

Yet in spite of the support of my appreciative students, my yoga community, and my guru, a nameless fear kept churning in my gut.

In September 1978, when Frank was about to turn nine, I went back to school to earn my master of social work degree at the University of Toronto. This two-year course, I reasoned, would help me work more effectively as a counsellor and in the new area of palliative care.

Once I graduated and rented a large space for a yoga classroom with a small adjoining office for counselling, I was on my way to becoming a social-work psychotherapist. Discovering Eugene Gendlin and Focusing in 1981 launched me personally and professionally on a path to self-discovery and authenticity. My goal in life became clear: to connect myself and others to our own deepest, wisest knowing.

Our society discourages us from valuing our visceral, animal body. Our heads are all-important. But Focusing teaches us to pay attention to our body's physically felt signals. No matter what situation we're in, the body is always responding. What our head knows is just the tip of the iceberg. Our real wisdom lies in the body.

Learning to ask my body how it felt and allowing its story to open up released a whole new, compassionate way of being with myself. I started to really like myself.

Inevitably, I uncovered, through Focusing, the cause of my strange fears. My struggle to live a normal life had its roots in child sexual abuse.

Part I of this book describes the darkness of my childhood suffering and my determined struggle to "fix" myself. Part II tells of my years of maturing through yoga and how, thanks to Focusing, I finally learned to accept my imperfect but authentic self. Part III describes how I found my lost childhood memories and how, with them, I found my own strength and purpose in life. I became a trauma therapist, as well as the founder and director of the Centre for Focusing, experiencing a joy and lightness I never could have imagined.

For the most part I tell my story chronologically, except where I describe scenes from the past that gradually came back to me—scenes from a childhood that I had completely forgotten.

I have to say that with the help of caring friends, a steadfastly loyal and loving husband, a wise and wonderful son, exceptional teachers, plus a determination to find help wherever I could, I have become one happy woman. Now, with this book, I want to share my knowledge and my hope. There is a way to recover from devastating trauma. Working through the pain and digging up the memories can lead to joy.

Acknowledgments

Without the support and guidance of my good friend Judy Steed, this book would never have been written. She is a veteran journalist and author of four of her own books, including *Our Little Secret: Confronting Child Sexual Abuse in Canada*. From the beginning, during the lonely days when I was first attempting to put my life experience into words, her encouragement and editing skills were my constant companions. Judy believed in my book. She believed from the start that it was my gift to the world—that it had to be sent out to the world.

PART 1

Trapped in a Fog

Chapter 1

In the Beginning

Looking at me during my childhood years you would have seen a spoiled rich kid always smiling and never causing any trouble. On the inside, life was different. Under the placid exterior I existed in a wet, gray fog, never quite sure of what was happening around me.

My mother was disappointed when she gave birth to me, a girl. She had hoped to produce a son for my father. They already had a daughter, my sister. Never mind that my father didn't want any more kids. Maybe to get back at her and maybe because he didn't give a damn, he had planned to be at army reserve camp when I was born. However, our family doctor shamed him into sticking around for my arrival.

Once my mother and I came home from hospital to our home in Stratford, Ontario, my five-year-old sister began a hate campaign that lasted throughout my childhood. Being smarter and stronger than I, she perfected endless ways of tormenting me.

In one of her choice tortures, she straddled my helpless body as I lay face up on the floor, drooled a long string of spit over my horrified face, then slurped it up just in time. Another favourite was what she called the Chinese Burner. In this one, she twisted the skin on my arm in opposite directions until I screamed with pain.

My sister had been sent away to relatives when Mommy was pregnant. My sister found Mommy's big, fat, pregnant belly disgusting, and Mommy couldn't stand her little girl's revulsion. Nobody told my sister that a baby was on the way. At the end of her visit to an aunt and uncle, she returned home to find a howling infant in a crib taking up a lot of Mommy's time. I can understand why she hated me. What I can't understand is why the adults didn't stop her from torturing me.

My father had grown up in a fine old Ontario family. His grandfather, who had come to Canada from Bandon, Ireland, became a respected educator and, from 1874, headed what was then called the Ontario Institution for the Education of the Blind (now the W. Ross Macdonald School), a provincial institute in Brantford. Since teaching paid poorly, he determined that all of his children would be lawyers. His sons W.H. and A.T. practised together as high-profile lawyers around Osgoode Hall in Toronto. Another son became Chief Justice of British Columbia. This son's white clapboard house, known as the Judge's House, is still open to tourists in Victoria.

My lawyer grandfather, W.H., found engineering interesting and decided that two of his sons, including my father, would break away from the family tradition of being teachers and lawyers. My father was fascinated during his student days in civil engineering by the building of the Welland Canal and Ontario's new roads. He graduated in engineering in 1929, right into the Great Depression. No more roads, no more canals, no more of anything he was interested in.

Needing to earn a living, he went to work for Coca-Cola Canada as their first-ever engineer. His family was shocked. What a comedown. The rest of the family had been professionals for generations.

Because he found the big company headquarters in Toronto stressful, he and my mother decided on a quieter lifestyle in a small city. They opened a Coca-Cola plant in picturesque Stratford.

They bought an old house backing onto the Avon River. A small bottling plant was already attached to the back of the house. With a franchise from Coca-Cola Canada, they began building a business with a fleet of red trucks, an ever-expanding territory, and, finally, a red brick factory on the edge of town. Soft drinks were big sellers during the Depression. A five-cent bottle of Coke brought instant gratification to a cash-strapped society thirsty for some relief from the grayness of those years. My parents were soon enjoying an affluent lifestyle while their disapproving family members, whose stocks and savings had shrunk, were forced to sell their big homes.

My mother, for her part, had grown up in genteel poverty in Toronto. She was one of five children. Her mother was widowed at a young age and raised her family on her own. The children strove to maintain whatever social standing they could cling to. For my mother, moving to Stratford put her securely at the top of the social order where she felt she rightly belonged.

A year after I was born, Canada declared war and my father went overseas to fight Hitler. His father lived with us and took over as the man of the house. W.H., as everyone called Grandpa, once a prominent lawyer in Toronto, was now old and arthritic. He babysat me while my mother ran the plant.

Stratford is a small city of about thirty thousand people, located a two-hour drive west of Toronto. We lived in a century-old, white brick mansion that my mother decorated in superb taste. The walls of the vast gray and yellow living room showed off mural-sized paintings by Canadian artists. This long room was furnished in antiques and matching loveseats that my mother had discovered during her painstaking searches of junk shops and visits to auctions. Hugely pregnant with me (I was born at ten pounds, four ounces), my tiny mother was nevertheless up and down the ladders as she turned the stately old house into her dream home.

When I was born our household consisted of my mother, my father, my sister, my father's father, often my mother's mother, Emma the maid, as well as a gardener, Mr. Mets, who came daily but lived elsewhere. Various girls from the country served as nursemaids.

Anyone seeing Grandpa and me together in his downstairs library, where leather-bound books lined the walls, would have found the scene charming. As a little girl, I spent many hours a day with Grandpa while he was reading or playing Solitaire on his pedestal table. In my attempt to join him, although I had not yet learned to read, I would haul a huge tome off the shelf and pretend to be studying it. Every once in a while I would ask him the meaning of some nonsense word of many syllables.

Grandpa would observe me in all seriousness.

"How do you spell it, Mary Kay?"

I would list off a string of my favourite alphabet letters, and a serious discussion would ensue before Grandpa returned to reading his books.

Once a week Grandpa and I took a slow walk to the library: the old man with his fedora, walking cane, and an armful of four books, and the little girl with long blonde curly hair and a big bow tied at the back of her short dress. It must have been a touching sight. Grandpa always took out four new books a week.

My mother found winters in our huge, drafty old house difficult during the war years when my father was overseas in the army. She was often exhausted from feeding hunks of coal into the basement's gigantic furnace, then removing the clinkers (what was left once the coal had burned) with giant tongs.

On top of running such a large house she needed surgery in Toronto when I was five years old and my sister was ten. My grandmother took care of me while my mother recovered. My sister was sent to the elite Bishop Strachan School in Toronto as a boarder. Bishop Strachan was the socially correct school that my mother had longed to attend when she was a girl but that her widowed mother could not afford. This was the beginning of separate lives for my sister and me. Each year as September rolled around, she chose to return to her private-school home. As an adult I wonder what she was running from.

One winter my mother decided that she and Grandpa and I would close the big house with the long driveway and monstrous furnace and move into the Queens Hotel in town. Grandpa looked after me while she worked. We ate our meals in the hotel dining room. All I remember about the food is that I discovered scrambled eggs with ketchup, which I ate every day.

Travelling salesmen sat in big leather armchairs in the lobby reading their newspapers and hoping someone would talk to them. As a five-year-old I considered it my place to sit on their laps and entertain them. My mother was both amused and embarrassed. As she put it, she was forever dragging me off some man's lap.

Men. They held a special power in my family. Male doctors were especially important. It's not surprising that I married a doctor.

Doctors were the heroes of my childhood. A favourite family story sheds light on my fondness for physicians. When I was three and we were still living in our big white house, my mother set a frosted silver cocktail shaker on a low table while she went to the door to receive her guests. Curious, I opened the lid and tasted its contents. It was delicious: frothy, sweet, and lemony. I tipped it up and downed the whole thing. When my mother returned to the living room with her guests she followed a trail of vomit that I had left from one end of our palatial living room to the other. For the rest of that evening my mother's guests split their sides laughing over my drunken three-year-old clowning.

It was our family friend, Dr. Gordon Greaves, who cleaned me up and made certain I didn't fall asleep until I had recovered. And in the end it was Dr. Greaves who carried me to bed, tucked me in, and said good night. The message was ingrained for life. Doctors are good and take care of us.

During the war years my father managed to get home on leave nearly every Christmas. He did this by escorting German and Japanese prisoners of war who were being shipped to northern Canada. In his absence my mother kept his memory alive with photos of him, which we dutifully kissed every night before bed. Once Daddy came home we would all be wonderfully happy.

When he did actually appear I was thrilled by his strength and his size. He was a giant! I remember sitting with him by the Christmas tree. The lights were twinkling and presents surrounded the tree. A cheery fire in the fireplace warmed the room.

I couldn't have been happier. I was three or four years old.

⌇⌇⌇

God is a man, too. At Sunday school they told us that God sees everything we do. He sees the little sparrow fall. If God so loves the little things, I know he sees me, too, no matter where I am. In the tall, narrow downstairs washroom just inside the front door of our house, I pull down my underpants, flip up my skirt, and bend forward so God can have a good look at my bottom. I want God to know I love him. God is a man. Men love bottoms.

Chapter 2

My Life Goes on Without Me

I daydreamed my way through grade two, the year my
father came home from the war for good. Most of the time
I imagined being the queen of the fairies. The plots varied but
had one prevailing theme: I was the beautiful, dearly loved
queen who had the power to find answers to everyone's pain.
(Does that sound like the origins of a psychotherapist?)

Miss Finkbeiner, my teacher, was a spinster who lived with
her aged mother across the street from Avon Public School.
Dr. Greaves was not just a friend of our family but also the public health doctor who came to our school regularly. Everyone
knew Miss Finkbeiner was in love with Dr. Greaves. The day he
poked his head in the door of the grade two classroom, spotted
me, and said, "Oh, there's my little girlfriend, Mary Kay," I just
knew my teacher was now my jealous, lifelong enemy.

At home I played a game over and over. I lined up my huge
collection of dolls and stuffed animals. They became my pupils.

I was the teacher, scolding and punishing them for being so stupid. I yelled at them and shook them as hard as I could. Nobody clued into my rage, although my mother did find my behaviour puzzling since I was never strapped or yelled at in school.

Most years my marks were mediocre. I never caused anyone any trouble, yet the teachers didn't like me. I guess they liked the bright kids who put their hands up a lot and got good marks. Maybe they tested intelligence in those days and figured I was just out to frustrate them. Whatever the truth, my parents considered me "sweet but not very bright." They said they did their best not to compare me with my clever older sister and to accept me for who I was.

I wasn't popular with the other children in my class either. I always felt strangely different from them. My mother said that if we lived in Toronto I wouldn't even know these children. They were "common." I would attend Bishop Strachan School with children from "better families."

Another daydream comforted me. In this fantasy I imagined a sort of inspector who came to our classroom to examine the children's clothing. He nods approvingly at my leather gloves (too expensive for a child, my mother said) and notes that my shoes are sturdy Oxfords, which are proper for a child's growing feet—not those cheap, fancy shoes some of the other girls wear.

What was the matter with me when I was seven and eight? I've looked for clues in some of my old report cards from early public school. I hoped for hints about my life during the years just after my father came back from the war. There was nothing unusual about my marks. They were pretty average, although teachers usually noted that I wasn't performing to my ability. I'm not surprised. I remember being scolded repeatedly for daydreaming and looking out the window. "Why can't you keep your mind on what you are supposed to be doing?" they asked.

"Mary's always daydreaming," my mother often mused. It was just something I did—part of my personality—and it wasn't a good character trait. It was something I needed to change. But I couldn't.

I had no idea why my head fogged over and my body went numb every time I needed to think. I just knew I couldn't shake my head clear to focus on long division or memorizing verses from the Bible.

There was another frequent remark on the report cards that I hadn't expected. Each teacher noted that I had missed too many half days of school. Half days? I let my mind drift back to those early grades and recall how I would often stay home because I wasn't feeling well. I wasn't malingering. I really didn't feel well. The centre of my body was a swamp of queasy, sick feelings. My head was fogged over. How could I face the demands of school with a dead head and a body carved out of rotting wood?

If I stayed home I could comfort myself by entering my imaginary realm where I was the queen of the fairies. There, with wisdom and sweet reason, I set about solving the problems of the other inhabitants of that world. Once we were all happy the swamp in my abdomen dried up and the fog in my head cleared. By afternoon I was well enough to go to school.

The world of the fairies was a seductive one. I tried hard to be a good girl and not slip away to that place, but when pressures arose in the classroom I was helplessly pulled down into that soft, padded world where instead of being clumsy and overweight I was the light, agile queen whose brain could solve anyone's problem and whose heart could bring peace to any conflict.

My parents thought I was a very calm child. "Mary Kay's not afraid of anything," they would boast. Little did they realize that at the slightest hint of danger I jumped inside myself where nothing could get to me and where I wouldn't even know what was happening. Of course I didn't squeal or tremble. I was frozen. Somehow their parental eyes did not recognize the signs of trauma.

I still have a photograph of myself, at about seven years of age, shopping in Toronto with my mother and sister. In the forties, when not everyone owned a camera, street photographers made a living snapping pictures of passersby. Once they had developed the photographs, they mailed them to their subjects.

My mother must have agreed to pay, because there we are, my mother, my sister, and I, walking along Bloor Street. In the picture, my mother and my sister are striding along, oblivious to the photographer's presence. My mother is wearing a tall hat that no doubt is meant to add stature to her five feet. Two fox skins, complete with little heads, hang around her neck to her waist, their glassy eyes staring at the sidewalk.

As for me, I am the poster child of post-traumatic stress disorder. My neck is pulled down into my torso. My left hand is making its way to my frightened face. My eyes are wide with fear, expecting something awful to happen. The photographer has caught me at the very moment that I am disappearing inside myself.

I don't want to give the impression that my whole childhood was spent in a fog. There were times when I came alive.

During the war years my mother designed and had built a swimming pool on our two acres of property. She had it dug into a hillside, which provided a natural deep end and drainage into a ditch. Over the diving platform an apple tree spread its shade. Children from all over the city came to our pool. Often it was too crowded for a young one like me, but I soon found a way to solve that problem. I would find a snake in the field surrounding the pool and dangle it over the throng of swimmers.

Everyone would scramble out and stand at the sides screaming, leaving the pool to my snake and me.

One of the times my father left for the war, he gave my mother money to buy herself a fur coat. Instead of heading to a furrier's she bought a black and white Springer Spaniel, her "fur on the hoof," as she called him. The dog had been the companion of a soldier who had been shipped overseas. It was not the sort of dog she intended to buy, but he put his paws on her short frame, pleading with his soft eyes for her to take him home. Her heart melted. She could not bear to leave him in the kennel.

That evening when my mother set the table for dinner we were all surprised to find the dog sitting on a chair at one of the places. He certainly *had* been the soldier's buddy. The dog didn't respond to the name my mother had picked for him, but she noticed that he became very attentive when she mentioned a zipper in conversation. She tried the word again and sure enough, that was his name.

Zipper was devoted to me. We spent many happy hours together. Being with Zipper was one of the best parts of my young life.

Dogs roamed freely in our small city. I remember my mother groaning at the sight of yet another pup that looked like Zipper. Irate townspeople frequently called and asked her to keep her male inside when their bitches were in heat. No matter how my mother tried to confine him, Zipper always managed to break out of the house when he picked up the scent of a female in heat.

I knew what she meant about pups looking like Zipper, but I was hoping she would explain some facts of life to me. "Zipper's a male. He can't be the mother of that pup," I said, pretending complete ignorance of the male role in procreation.

Instead of taking the opportunity to educate me, she ended the discussion by saying, "Oh yes, of course. You're right."

Zipper saw it as his duty to escort me to school each morning and afternoon and to wait for me at lunchtime and after school. After being chased off the school grounds a number of times by the caretaker, he took up his post each day across the road from the school. How did he know when it was three-thirty? I don't know. But he never failed to accompany me to and from school.

One time when Zipper and I were roaming the neighbourhood together I had a dramatic experience of what humans are capable of if they're frightened enough.

Many of the neighbours across the street shared a large communal vegetable garden in the field behind their houses. Mrs. Chisolm was one of these keen gardeners. Apparently Zipper had been running through her tomato plants. Maybe he'd also been lying on her green beans. In any case she came running after him with a long plant stake, shouting and threatening to kill him.

I was terrified. An attack on Zipper was an attack on me. I ran to hide in the next-door garage, realized I was trapped there, and—before registering what I was doing—I jumped through the high garage window to escape. Did some part of me notice that it had no glass? Would I have jumped through anyway? The amazing thing is that there is no way I should have been able to jump through that window. I was a chubby kid and not given to athletic feats.

Zipper and I loved and understood each other. He was always there to comfort me ... but not for long. We went away on holiday one summer and when we returned, he was no longer there. He'd had a tumour on his head and apparently my mother had asked the veterinarian to put him out of his misery. My mother loved Zipper, too, and his death became another of those mysterious matters "we do not talk about." I grieved for him alone. I was just starting grade three.

Besides Zipper, the only one who loved me and thought I was special was my maternal grandmother. On her frequent visits I curled up on her lap or snuggled with her in bed. When she stayed at our house I felt safe and happy. She died the same year as Zipper. Morning after morning I was sure she was sitting on the side of my bed. But as soon as I opened my eyes she was gone. To this day I do not know what to make of that sense of her presence.

My mother was very close to her mother. She went into mourning when her mother died but never let me see her grieve. I thought I was the only one who was heartbroken. I had nobody to talk to about my grief. I was kept from the funeral and any expression of sadness.

At my mother's invitation our minister came to our house to talk to me. He asked me if I had any questions for him. Questions? My heart was broken. What sort of questions could possibly help? But I tried to appease my mother's expectations by asking him some goofy things like "Do they roller skate in heaven?" And "Do they eat ice cream in heaven?" I knew this wasn't what was expected of me but it was the best I could do. The minister and my mother gave me withering smiles. He instructed my mother and me to kneel in prayer at the coffee table and he intoned some "soothing words." When he finally left, my mother abandoned me in disgust. I could return to crying for my grandmother without the intrusion of adults.

If grade two had been painful, grade three was worse. Now, instead of Miss Finkbeiner, Mrs. Babensee was my teacher. Her classroom was in the dreary basement of our overcrowded school. Like Miss Finkbeiner she was fond of the cute, smart kids. This was the year I was kept back with the "dumb bunnies." It was also the year my beloved grandmother died. With the fog in my head even thicker, I struggled just to figure out what was happening around me. The teacher's instructions, the chatter of my fellow pupils, the expectation to look like everybody else at recess and during gym class: All of these things were hopelessly confusing to me.

I was very awkward. Baseball was central to our outdoor activities, but I was too fat to run the bases. Usually I was placed out in left field, only to realize, when a ball finally flew my way, that I'd been daydreaming again.

I liked skating so my mother signed me up for figure skating after school on Tuesdays. She even paid for private lessons. This led to another humiliation. During those lessons I was required to cut a neat figure eight on the ice. The male pro made no attempt to hide his disdain for the sloppy figures I carved into the pristine ice with the blades of my white figure skates.

"No, no, no," he would yell in the cold, hollow space of the arena. "It's an eight, not some wobbly, ugly thing."

Worse, my mother, huddled in her fur coat, was watching from the bleachers. I really liked skating, except for the lessons. In fact I continued skating once I was well into my adulthood and became a really good recreational skater.

My mother encouraged me to exercise. She signed me up for gymnastics on Saturday mornings. This led to more embarrassment. There was no way I could hoist my fat body over the high leather horse in the centre of the gymnasium.

Perhaps to make up for my lack of physical competence, I was a bossy kid. In my favourite activities, I was always the leader. When my best friend, Charron, and I organized the little kids for summertime games and activities, I was the boss. At ages seven and eight, as an avid reader of the *Polly Pigtails' Magazine for Girls*, I founded and presided over the Polly Pigtails Club. You had to wear pigtails to be accepted as a member. This was no problem for the gang of little girls who settled into the red leather sofas and chairs in my father's den as I called the meeting to order. We all wore pigtails anyway or had hair long enough to braid for the meetings.

When Johnny, the little kid across the road, got wind of the club, he wanted to join. We explained that he needed braids, but he was adamant. He refused to be left out. In the end I found some bright yellow wool and braided yellow pigtails to hang on either side of his round face. I can still see my father's face peeking around the doorframe during our meetings. He found the sight of Johnny in yellow pigtails hilarious. It was the first time I heard the word "blackmail" as my father joked about having something on Johnny that he could use later in life.

I recall telling Charron that when I grew up I wanted to be a woman who gave speeches about important things. Of course I had no idea *what* I would be talking about as an adult. Interestingly, to this day my sense of myself as a professional adult is similar to the feeling I enjoyed as president of the Polly Pigtails Club. I thrive on making good things happen. My years of teaching and hosting workshops as a yoga teacher and as the founder and director of the Centre for Focusing, of giving talks, workshops, and training seminars in Toronto, the U.S., and Europe: Did all of that grow from the seeds of my club?

Chapter 3

When Father Came Marching Home

In 1945, when I was seven, the war ended and the men came home. What a strange time for the world. It was an era of men with post-traumatic stress disorders caused by the horrors of war. And for many couples it was a time of marital stress from too many years of living separate lives.

I don't know how my parents' marriage would have been different if it hadn't been interrupted by the war. And I don't know if my father would have relied less on rye whisky and Coke to face his world. He had always been a party boy, but after the war he was seldom sober.

Each time he returned home during the war years I had initially been scared of him. He was huge. He could lift me up with one hand. Mostly I remember his smell. It was different from anyone else's: a nose-tingling blend of the rough khaki wool of his scratchy uniform, the whisky on his breath, and the ever-present Export A in his mouth.

Once he had been with us for a day or two, though, my shyness faded and I delighted in climbing onto his giant lap.

When he returned home for good I experienced a strange mixture of fear and intense love. I wanted to be with him as much as possible. The most important thing in my young life was keeping Daddy happy. (Many years later, I learned he had taken up with another woman when he was in England. My role in the family, at least as my mother saw it, had been to keep him home with us in Canada.)

I grew up believing I was very fortunate to be my father's companion. I thought I was lucky to go off camping with him, just the two of us. Tales of our trips became part of our family lore—we all relished the stories of the adventures of Daddy and Mary Kay.

My father often made up heroic tales about himself and promised that he and I would have wild adventures together. Being only seven years old, I didn't recognize the grandiosity of an alcoholic in the manic stage of a bipolar disorder. Later I came to recognize the signs: His mouth would twist to one side as he strained to enunciate words, with ugly throat squeaks coming out instead of intelligible sounds. His blue eyes bulged as he struggled to speak, cigarette ash dangling dangerously at the end of his Export A.

My father promised to take me camping when I learned to scrub a frying pan. This was a favourite story in my family. Here's how I recall the event.

One day in August, that year when I was seven, my father returned home for dinner from the Coca-Cola plant following his routine stop for drinks at the officers' mess. Parking his Plymouth Coupe behind our house, he found me on the back porch scrubbing the last of the frying pans I had gathered to show him. He didn't look pleased and walked away. I could hear him talking to my mother in the kitchen. She must have told him he had to keep his promise to a child. A few minutes later he returned, laughing, to assure me that he would take me after all.

Soon after, the two of us piled into his car and drove to Muskoka in Ontario's cottage country while my mother and sister took off for Bigwin Inn, a fashionable resort in the area.

I was aware and at the same time wasn't aware that my father's frequent stops to open the trunk of the car were making him more and more drunk. He kept a red metal Coke cooler there containing a block of ice and glass bottles of Coke. He would drink a bit from a bottle, pour in a belt of rye, and continue sipping and driving until the next stop.

The more he drank, the more my head fuzzed over. That's how my brain protected me from being terrified of the danger I was in, driving with this drunken protector. In fact I was angry with people along the way who snickered at his slurred speech and wobbly gait. It never occurred to me to be mad at him. I realize now that the amused stares of those passersby threatened to pry open my reality: that I was with a man who was not a proper guardian for a child.

I remember being embarrassed by his attempts to impress the blonde waitress at the soda counter in the Port Carling drugstore. I wanted to explain to her that my father was really a very nice man. And when we stayed overnight at the cottage of one of my mother's friends I resented her for wanting to take care of me. Her solicitous attention made it clear she considered my father an unsuitable caregiver for a seven-year-old child.

What on earth was my mother thinking when she waved us off on our camping trip? Didn't she realize my father was driving drunkenly around the country with me in the passenger seat? How could she have sent us off together?

Once we rented our canoe and set out for our camping trip, we were free of censuring eyes. The canoe was red. We had a tent and sleeping bags and enough groceries to last a week. And of course we had a frying pan. We finally made camp on deserted Flower Island. My father set up the tent and cooked our meal. He had brought groundsheets and explained that we could sleep under the stars if we put the groundsheets under us to keep out the damp. We bedded down on a velvety August night with the stars so close and bright you could almost touch them.

Hours later I wakened to the sound of my father's snoring. I lay there in the dark, looking up. "Oh no!" I thought. "The sky is falling." It was like the story of Henny Penny who tricked herself into believing the sky was falling down, except now it really was happening. I lay there stiff with fear. One after the other, stars shot across the sky and fell. We were going to die. Should I wake my father or just let him sleep through the end of the world? It would be kinder to let him sleep. But when I grew so terrified that I could no longer bear it alone I shook him awake and told him what was happening. His response was gentle and reassuring. He patiently explained to me about falling stars, comets, meteors, more than I ever needed to hear, until I fell asleep.

My mother liked to tell the story of sunning with my sister on the dock at Bigwin Inn when she saw a red canoe in the distance.

"That's your father and your sister out there," she said as she pointed towards the canoe.

"Oh Mother, you can't tell from here."

"Oh yes I can. There's a big one in the stern and a little one in the bow who's doing all the work. That would be your father and Mary Kay." And of course it was.

After roughing it in our sleeping bags for a couple of days, my father and I settled into the luxury of the Bigwin Inn, and for a few days I once again became a child and not my father's companion.

Some years later my father and I drove to Owen Sound to catch a ferry to Manitoulin Island. We stayed at an inn there that turned out to be owned by my father's old public-school friend. The owner and his wife welcomed us, but I could see they were uncomfortable with my father's drinking. Again this made me uneasy. I didn't want them to notice his drunkenness.

It would have been natural for me to feel anxious being alone with my drunken father and driving the north's twisting roads with him. But it is not fear that stands out in my memory. It is only embarrassment and anger.

We left the inn and any prying eyes when we hired a seaplane and a Native guide, Norman. Once we had left the resort I forgot there was anything abnormal in a father and daughter going off on a fishing trip. Norman set up camp on an isolated island and we went fishing. He strung the fish through their gills on a metal stringer and cooked all our meals. As we gradually ate the fish on the stringer, Norman cut off their bodies, leaving their heads attached. Everywhere we paddled, that school of dismembered heads trailed behind our canoe. I was mesmerized by the grizzly sight.

I felt shy with Norman, but honoured to be in the company of a real member of the First Nations. He revealed that he had a wife and baby. I tried hard to imagine what it would be like to live in one of those small cabins I had seen on Manitoulin Island where he and other First Nations people lived with their families.

My father treated Norman with great respect. My father's father had befriended the famous Oronhyatekha (aka Peter Grant) and as a result had done legal work for the Six Nations. Oronhyatekha had grown up in an age of racism but nonetheless studied at Oxford University and then graduated as a physician from the University of Toronto. He later joined the international, whites-only fraternal organization, the Independent Order of Foresters, in 1878 and held the top post of Supreme Chief Ranger (now International Fraternal President), a position my grandfather later occupied. So my father's history with the First Nations ran deep.

When we returned to the inn my father invited Norman to our room. He poured him rye whisky and when it came time for Norman to leave, it became apparent he was staggeringly drunk. I felt the sadness of this. Norman, I realized, was not accustomed to rye the way my father was.

Often my father took me on trips around Muskoka, usually to cottages of friends. I was so lucky to have a father who took me camping and to cottage country, friends would remark. In some ways I had succeeded in becoming the boy my mother wanted for my father.

It was on one of those northern camping trips that I heard my first loon. Again we were sleeping under the stars and my father was snoring peacefully. In the pitch black night, the loons' crazy laughter rang out as they called to one another. As with the Henny Penny experience I lay there frightened for what seemed like hours before waking my sleeping father. Again he was patient with me as he explained what I was hearing.

I snuggled back into my sleeping bag, trusting in my father to keep me safe.

I adored my father and my father adored me. That's what my mother said and that's what I believed.

When we were at home in the city, every night after dinner I climbed onto my father's lap to cuddle and entertain him. The rest of the family and whoever was present as a guest would smile at our wonderful, happy relationship. I remember the softness of his body, layered with more and more soft fat as the years melted away the army's toughening. I breathed in his wonderful smell. He smelled better than anybody in the whole world. I worked hard to make him laugh. When he laughed, everybody was happy.

My parents were keen bridge players. I entertained their friends, much to my father's delight. One evening, before I was sent upstairs to bed, a red-faced man with a big tummy asked me: "Who do you like best to go places with, your mother or your father?"

"My father," I replied.

"Why?"

"My mother often forgets her purse, but my father never forgets his pants."

The red-faced man turned even redder as he doubled over in spasms of laughter. My father couldn't have been more delighted. He hugged me and kissed me and sent me off to bed.

Chapter 4

Trapped

Grade three was the year the class was divided into two. Smart kids got to do grade four work, skipping a grade. Dumb kids sat in separate rows doing grade three stuff. I was held back with the dumb kids.

I dreaded telling my parents. Standing in front of them that evening I looked for a way to soften the blow.

"Well," I assured them, "I'm the smartest of the dumb bunnies."

My father doubled over, his smoker's cough erupting. That was the funniest thing he'd ever heard. Smartest of the dumb bunnies! Ha, ha, ha!

My mother shared his amusement, albeit less raucously.

As for me I just slunk away, relieved they weren't mad at me. Nobody ever asked me how *I* felt about it. In fact I don't remember my parents ever mentioning it again.

My friends went on with the smart kids and I stayed behind.

By the time I got to high school, I was already older and feeling more sophisticated than my classmates, especially the late-maturing boys. When I was sixteen I tried to make up for the lag by choosing an older boyfriend. His interest in me may have soothed one part of my battered ego, but the fact that I couldn't say no to his sexual urges made me feel even worse about myself. This was the fifties and only bad girls had sex with their boyfriends. It wasn't that I wanted sex. I was simply unable to say "no" to anyone else's needs. The only thing I was good at was making everybody else feel happy.

My shame became unbearable when I actually failed grade eleven. I couldn't believe it. I was a real dud. Sure I spent too much time skipping classes and hanging out in the highway restaurant where the cool kids gathered, but even that didn't explain why I had failed.

My life was slipping out of my control. The worse it got the more my head fogged over. How could I face going back to my high school? I was already a year or two behind my friends. They'd gone on to nurses' training or university. My boyfriend, older than I, was working for a local finance company, lending money to people until their next paycheques. Sex was a service I performed for him. I certainly wasn't satisfying any sexual needs of my own.

In fact I was totally numb to what was going on "down there." When my family doctor referred to my vagina I had little idea what he was talking about and reported to my friends something about "my regina." I felt dirty and ashamed. I was becoming more and more mired in the ugliness and tawdriness of my existence. I could see no way out.

At last my guilt and anxiety grew intolerable when my boyfriend asked me to lend him the $100 I had saved. He promised to repay it promptly but failed to do so. I was desperately afraid my parents would find out. Somehow I had to get clean again. I had to get back my innocence.

I thought of Bishop Strachan School in Toronto, where my sister had spent so much of her childhood, the school my mother held in such high regard. I pleaded with my parents to let me go. Visions of those private school girls with their shining faces and, as I imagined, their pure, innocent souls, convinced me this was where I could get away from my predatory boyfriend, escape my parents' questions about the $100, and avoid facing classmates much younger than I. And I could get clean there. I would become someone else.

And so my mother drove me to Toronto for the interview that would determine whether I would be allowed inside the hallowed halls of Bishop Strachan. With its leaded windowpanes and Romanesque arches, it looked like a school for the privileged. I was determined they would admit me to that place of beautiful, innocent girls. I was escaping!

Once the fall came and I was a BSS student, I realized I had escaped the frying pan only to jump into the fire.

Changing schools hadn't solved the embarrassment of being the oldest in the class. The faces were different but my fellow students were still younger than I was. I wanted to be part of my school's next level, with girls my own age. That's where I felt I belonged.

Here I was, seventeen years old and not allowed to leave the school grounds unless I was on a school outing to the theatre or ballet. I couldn't believe it. I was a prisoner. My greatest act of rebellion was to lean out the window in the middle of the night to smoke a cigarette. Being caught would have meant expulsion, but I was desperate.

My Stratford boyfriend moved to Toronto. With the permission of my parents, he could call on me and take me out.

The irony of it! I could see Mrs. Rogers, the housemother, didn't think much of him. I even thought I saw her smirk when I introduced him to her as a friend of the family.

One good thing did happen. I auditioned for the school play and impressed the director so much that she seemed to be seriously considering me for the lead role. Then, I suspect, Mrs. Rogers had a word with her. There was no more mention of the heroine's part. Any interest I had in being a BSS girl was fast disappearing.

Christmas came and I returned home to Stratford for the holidays. I begged my parents not to send me back. They were adamant. My father had paid the whole year's fees. My mother said I had to give it a fair chance. I returned like a prisoner to maximum security.

One day, a month or so later, I couldn't stand it any longer. It was winter, so I could cover my school uniform with a coat. If I could make it off the school property, it wouldn't be obvious that I was a BSS student.

I headed for the taxi company nearby, telling the driver to take me to the train station. I'd hoped to take a train to Stratford. However, no trains were expected for many hours. I phoned my unsavoury boyfriend who came to "rescue" me. Naturally, we ended up in his apartment having sex before he took me back to prison where he presented himself as the responsible one. Somehow, my mother and her friend, Nora, appeared at the school soon after. What a remarkable coincidence. They must have been in Toronto for a theatre matinée.

I remember sitting in the housemother's suite when my mother and Nora arrived. I don't remember much of what followed. The women talked while I sat helpless to affect my fate. Whatever they decided would be what would happen to me. Then I recall returning briefly to my bedroom to pack my belongings. I was out of jail! I don't remember the drive home. I do remember walking in the front door of our house in Stratford.

My father greeted us at the door. His blue eyes were bleary and his speech slurred. He was drunk. He looked troubled. Oh no. I was the cause of his drinking. It was my fault that he was drunk.

Around this time, my sister, who had moved to Winnipeg, gave birth to her third son. My mother flew out to be with her. That left my father and me alone in the house, except for Pearl, the maid who came each morning and left before supper.

I was miserable living with my father, preparing his supper and generally being the woman of the house. I don't recall much of what went on during that time, except for memories of my father chewing at the dinner table with his mouth open. I wanted to scream with rage at him. Of course I did no such thing. I simply pouted and sighed.

At last my mother returned home from Winnipeg and life returned to what had seemed normal before my attempt to purify myself at Bishop Strachan School.

There is a final piece of irony about my attempts to leave BSS. One winter evening I happened to tell my mother about the housemother finding girls in each other's beds. Mrs. Rogers had created a flurry of excitement in the otherwise dreary nightlife of the school by storming in and out of bedrooms, asking each of us if we'd been guilty of physical intimacy with the other boarders.

My mother's reaction surprised me. If she'd known about sex among the boarders, she told me, she'd have removed me from the school right away!

I couldn't believe my ears. All along I'd had a means of escape available to me and I hadn't known.

During my years in high school, my big sister had been raising her children. She had eloped with her boyfriend when she was in grade twelve. Her twin boys were born when I was twelve and she was just seventeen. These tiny preemies needed all the help my sister could get for them. They were born in June and that summer, along with my mother, a maid, and my sister's husband, I took my turn in the nursery feeding, changing, and rocking the babies.

I never doubted my competence or my ability to look after them. Perhaps because I had always played with dolls, I was far more at ease than my sister with their frail little bodies. In those days, I thought they were the most wonderful beings ever and spent long hours playing with and caring for them.

During my teen years I took them with me whenever I could. We'd meet my friends and the twins would explain that they were "Mary's little monsters," never realizing the teenage sarcasm in their nickname. They knew I was crazy about them.

Their younger brother, who was born just after I escaped from BSS, was also very important to me. So was his sister, born a few years later. These children gave meaning to my life and gave me a strong sense of family.

If you'd asked me in those days whether I was happy, I probably would have answered yes. I loved my family. I had good friends. I drove around town in my father's flashy convertible. I had clothes that were stylish and tasteful. I didn't realize my head was in a fog. I knew no other way of being.

Chapter 5

Escaping

The year I attended grade thirteen my father became an invalid. He'd had surgery for a duodenal ulcer. A heart condition made him afraid to climb stairs or exert himself in any way. It became clear that he would live out his days on the ground floor, spending his time smoking and reading. *His* arthritic old father had died at eighty-six. *My* father seemed to be throwing in the towel early.

For Ontario students in the 1950s grade thirteen determined your future. No matter how dismal your earlier marks, if you did well in the last year you could go to university. I was desperate to get away from home. All my friends had graduated, leaving me with much younger classmates. Sitting on the curved bench of the bay window in my second-floor bedroom, I studied hard. My parents were offering me the apartment at the back of their house, and maybe a car, if only I'd stay home with them. I wanted to go to Ryerson and study journalism, but the school guidance counsellor, Davy Root, advised me to aim for a four-year honours course at the University of Toronto. As he explained it to me, I'd likely be meeting my future husband in the next few years. At the university I'd meet "a better class of people."

Airhead that I was I nodded and set about filling out my application for a four-year honours course in Modern Languages and Literature. In hindsight I see I was much more suited to the stimulating world of journalism than the academic halls of a world-class university.

Once the letter came from the University of Toronto saying I had been accepted my mother began taking me on shopping trips to nearby London, where we bought the necessary fashionable outfits for starting university. I vividly remember hunting for the smart clothes that would prepare me for campus life. I still have an old copy of *The Varsity*, the university newspaper, with a picture of me, a well-dressed freshman, walking through the arch of the Soldiers' Tower at Hart House on the University of Toronto campus.

My parents drove me to Toronto and installed me on the third floor of the Whitney Hall residence overlooking St. George Street with its constant buzz of traffic, ambulances, and shouting students. The first week I thought the noise would drive me crazy. By the second week I no longer noticed the cacophony of the big city. I'd developed an urban dweller's noise filters. I relished the anonymity of being able to go downtown without meeting anyone I knew. The sense of freedom was exhilarating.

Once I left home and entered the world of the university, my life changed dramatically. True, I spent endless hours lying on my bed, smoking and sleeping. But my head was beginning to clear and some intellectual ideas were actually grabbing my attention. In fact the longer I stayed away from my family the smarter I became. Studying Emerson and Thoreau, the American transcendentalists, infused me with a taste for the views of their spiritual descendants, the Unitarian Universalists. Today, as a mature woman, my church, the First Unitarian Congregation of Toronto, is central to my life.

University was also the time when I met many of the people who are still my close friends today. My roommate was Sue Hamilton Van Iterson, whose family lived in Toronto. If she were Jewish and a male she'd be called a *mensch*, that wonderful Yiddish term for someone who is good, kind, decent, and honourable.

I was fascinated with the way Sue could stand up for herself or offer a different slant on an issue without seeming rude or angry. She simply stated her well-considered opinion and was comfortable doing so.

Night after night Sue and I lay awake at opposite ends of our long, narrow residence room with its posters on the walls, two desks, and two dressers, and talked about our lives and our families. I told her about my perfect family: how my mother was beautiful and clever, my father wise and witty. They were the perfect couple. Sue heard all about my aunts, uncles, nephews, and the characters who peopled my hometown. My idealized family was glamorous and gifted.

Sue talked about her family, too. She described them as decent people with some problems, not nearly as extraordinary as the family I presented. She described her relationship with her mother as happy and loving. Sue's family was a functional one, something I couldn't recognize at the time.

Sue taught me how to iron a blouse since our maid had always pressed my clothes at home. Sue's offer to demonstrate the fine art of shirt laundering followed my first adult experience with the emotion of anger. I had sulked or pouted in the past, but anger's powerful rush of energy was a new experience.

I had sent a shirt out for laundering and it came back dry cleaned. I was furious! It had cost more to dry clean and they may have ruined my it by not washing it. Even as I was cursing the cleaners, I was intrigued and curious about what was happening in my body. Powerful, uncomfortable surges of energy were coursing through my gut. My legs were quivering and my face was flushed. I watched, alarmed and intrigued. So this is what anger feels like! It was a strange new power. One part of me liked the sense of being alive. The other feared what would happen if I actually started reacting emotionally to the world around me. I would no longer appear calm and in charge, that was for sure.

<hr>

My new boyfriend, Harvey, was also having a strange—but quite different—effect on me. Inside, I'd always felt like a sensible gray flannel suit. But now my insides had changed to shimmering, flashing taffeta or soft gossamer blowing in a gentle breeze. I felt all the emotions around me, including my own. I was like a running stream of sensations and thoughts. Colours were brighter. Sounds resonated in my head and body. Life was rich and overflowing with meaning.

I met Harvey on my first day at university. He wasn't the promising young man from an affluent family my mother, the guidance counsellor, and I had hoped for. In fact he lived over an accordion academy in the Little Italy area of Toronto with his mother and siblings and drove a funny little Morris Minor, which he kept operational by buying wrecks for parts. The car was pink, held together by piano wire, and had a see-through patch on the floor under which the road sped by. Harvey started it by jumping out of the driver's seat, running around to the front, and turning a crank.

Harvey's dream was to become a physician. To make enough money to stay in school, he worked at Canada Packers, carrying butchered bull fronts on his strong back. Then he would sit in class during the day, often falling asleep from sheer exhaustion. When I met him he was in his second year of physical education. He'd chosen it so that, at the end of three years, he could get out and teach. That would make him enough money to continue later with medical school. As it turned out he didn't have to teach. When Harvey graduated, Dr. Harry Ebbs, the head of the School of Physical and Health Education, recognized his special qualities and arranged for a scholarship so he could enter medical school directly.

I was in awe of Harvey's determination. My parents paid my fees and my living expenses and provided me with spending money. I was just a spoiled rich kid looking for a husband. I had no realistic vision of what my future held. All I knew was that I wanted to travel. I longed to live and work in Europe, probably in France. Daydreams and fantasies had me using my education in modern languages and literature to get a highly paid and prestigious post in some European embassy. At other times I imagined myself married to an incredibly wealthy and adoring man. Of course we would travel widely and often.

Harvey talked about doing *good* in the world. He was born in 1936 in Malaysia to a father who was a tropical horticulturalist and a mother who was the daughter of a famous Scottish politician. His culturally aware father began to notice that the sandals on the feet of men in the market were Japanese, not Malay. This could only mean that the Japanese were infiltrating the country in preparation for an invasion. He arranged to take a leave of absence from work and took his family to England when Harvey was six months old. Of course, by the time the war started, the Japanese were well in place in Britain's southeast Asian colonies.

The family then moved to Guatemala where Harvey's father's next job was attempting to grow quinine. The U.S. State Department figured the coming war would be fought in the South Pacific. They needed quinine to fight malaria. Harvey's father arranged for cinchona seedlings, from which quinine was made, to be stolen from the Dutch in Java, Indonesia, because the Dutch were not sharing their effective anti-malarial medicine with the rest of the world.

From Guatemala the family moved to the Dominican Republic, where they lived on a remote sugar plantation surrounded by a highly structured community of white Americans, Spaniards, professional Dominicans, and workers from various social classes. Socializing between classes was not acceptable.

By the time I met Harvey at university he was attending his twenty-eighth school. He'd gone to school in San Juan, Puerto Rico, where his mother rented an apartment for herself and her four children during the school year so they would get an education. He and his older brother also went to Munro College in Jamaica where Harvey had the mind-opening experience of sharing a dorm with a black boy. At Munro colour made no difference. This was a real—and lasting—cultural lesson for Harvey. Before, in the Dominican Republic, he and the black boy who had served as his caddy on the golf course had started playing together, looking for golf balls lost in the stream or the woods. In that race-conscious country, nothing was said to Harvey. He was white and therefore not to blame. But the black boy was punished.

Harvey witnessed incredible poverty in the Caribbean. He felt the injustice and knew how hard it was for people working on the plantation to get enough to eat. Harvey's father was criticized for causing dissatisfaction among other workers. His sin? He had provided extra rice for his men to take home to their families.

Harvey spent time with the wise old black men on the plantation. The blacksmith showed him how to hold hot coals in his hands without getting burned. Workers in the field brought him baby birds from the sugar cane fields when cane-cutting frightened away their parents and left them helpless. Harvey started a bird hospital and taught the baby birds how to catch lizards before setting them free. It was his first experience in running a hospital.

When Harvey and I became friends he would talk about all the countries he had lived in. In his most recent adventure, his family had been forced to leave the Dominican Republic. Rafael Trujillo, the cruel dictator, had nationalized the sugar industry and ejected all foreigners from the country. As Harvey recounted his memories of that time I felt a shudder of fear. He told me the terror of Trujillo's reign sometimes followed people to North America. And in the Dominican Republic, if Trujillo coveted your house or your daughter, they were his.

Canada, with no draft to force young men into the armed forces, seemed a good choice for a family with three boys, but it didn't work out for their father. There was precious little work for a tropical horticulturist in this northern country. After working as a janitor to put food on the table he finally gave up trying to find work in Canada and was hired to oversee a rubber plantation in Brazil.

Harvey's mother went to work as a stenographer, using the shorthand she'd learned as her politician father's assistant in the days when the two of them had travelled together throughout his constituency in Scotland.

Harvey's father died the first year we were married. He was only fifty-six when he succumbed to a gastrointestinal infection in a remote part of Brazil that lacked even basic medical care.

I was fascinated by Harvey's background. After all that's what I wanted to do—travel and have adventures. I fell in love with this man and knew I wanted to spend my life with him. Of course we would travel and travel, I thought. What I didn't realize was that, as Harvey was falling in love with me, he was imagining roots and stability. He was marrying a local girl with a family who had lived in Canada for generations. He would never travel again, he was telling himself. His wandering days were over.

The problem was, we didn't tell each other our dreams.

I look back on those days before the birth control pill changed sexual morality, those days when we were hopelessly in love, needing to be together, yet kept apart by society's ban on sex before marriage. Unmarried sex was only for bohemians and bad girls. When Harvey was in his second year of medical school and I had a year remaining at university, I realized I was pregnant. We'd get married, but that would mean the end of Harvey's dream of becoming a physician. I knew he'd always feel cheated out of his dream if he couldn't complete his training.

In the end we decided I would confide in my mother and ask for her help. Maybe she'd convince my father to finance us so we could get married and have the baby. Once I graduated I could make good money teaching in a high school, enough to look after the baby and help Harvey get through his training. We were only asking for one year's help. It seemed perfectly reasonable to us.

My mother's reply was swift and harsh. No, she wouldn't tell my father. I was to drink castor oil until I aborted. She didn't want to hear about my pregnancy ever again.

Harvey and I got married in a civil ceremony at City Hall with a few friends. In a time when abortion was a crime, Harvey found a kind and competent doctor to perform the procedure. I have never stopped grieving for that baby.

Once I graduated from university I landed a contract for what seemed a huge amount of money teaching high school English. This was not my dream job by any means but I could fulfill my agreement to support us while Harvey studied.

Being a first-year teacher is tough at the best of times. Being a first-year teacher who has just married, whose head fuzzes over so she can't think, and whose husband is angry and disappointed with her performance as a wife, is hell. Many mornings my frightened stomach threw up its breakfast. Driving out to the suburbs to teach was a daily act of courage. Adolescents can quickly sniff out a teacher's fear and they soon caught the scent of my distress. I was failing in adulthood and I was failing in marriage. The fears I'd been pushing down my whole life were breaking through.

I wasn't the happy, loving wife Harvey had expected. Most of the time I was either frightened or numb. Harvey knew I was bright, but somehow I never remembered or seemed interested in what he told me. For him it was emotional abandonment. Yet how could I be empathic when most of the time I was dead inside? Once he entered psychiatric training he found a cruel label to fit my behaviour. I was "passive aggressive." The diagnosis was technically correct, I realize now. It did nothing at the time, however, to capture the agony of numbness and depression I was experiencing.

To be fair to Harvey, I was hard to live with. I assured him at one moment that I loved him, wanted to be close to him, and would care for him. The next moment I was lost in my black hole of isolating despair.

To be fair to *me*, I had no idea why I found it impossible on some days to carry out ordinary acts, why love-making often seemed repugnant, why I agreed to a task and then put it off indefinitely, or why I shut down and let nobody near me, replacing any openness with tight shoulders and a bright smile.

Life was closing in on me in my struggle to shelter myself from a scary world.

I had a recurring nightmares about finding hundreds of newborn babies in my bed. In the dream I was frantically trying to keep some of them alive. I would rush to save one and another would die. The babies felt like my dying dreams for myself.

There was always the deadening, heavy weight in my stomach and the need to build a wall against whatever it was I was afraid of. What *was* I so afraid of? I didn't know. It kept changing. Some logical part of me searched for a rational explanation to justify the fear that upset my gut and tightened my neck and shoulders into spasms of pain.

Some days I'd identify a particular person I was afraid to meet if I left the house. Other times I'd be walking around carrying my maximum load of stress when I'd see someone I recognized. Anybody! My body's hair-trigger pistol would fire, my lips would twitch nervously, and I'd be too scared to speak. I'm sure my eyes were saucer-wide as I stood helplessly humiliated and exposed before the object of my terror. The worst part was my embarrassment. No matter how I felt inside, I needed to look good to the outside world. That is what mattered.

I developed a phobia about my hometown. It made no sense, but whenever I met someone from Stratford in Toronto or had to travel to Stratford to visit my parents, I panicked.

Where had she gone, that intelligent girl with the bright future and the great wardrobe—the person I'd been in university? The young woman who had loved and was loved until she married? Sex had been exciting, friends had surrounded me, the man I loved wanted me passionately. Now I was a tight bundle of anxiety, afraid of everything, not daring to reach out to life. I did what many depressed people do: I found comfort in picking an early age for my death. I believed I wouldn't live past twenty-eight. To live longer than that was just too painful to contemplate.

PART II

Struggling to Survive

Chapter 6

Yoga and Me

By 1964 Harvey had finished medical school and was working long hours as a junior intern at Toronto General Hospital, moving ahead with his dream of becoming a doctor. As for me I was stuck in an emotional black hole, too scared to expose myself to the adult world. I was trained as a high school teacher, but the strange fear that made my body shake and my head go numb had forced me to give up my job as well as my post-graduate studies in Italian. I simply couldn't function anywhere that observing eyes might view me critically. Shame and humiliation clouded my days. Worse, my fears made no sense. What did I have to be so frightened about?

I rarely saw Harvey, and when I did, he was exhausted from the inhumane sleepless nights of on-call interns. We lived in subsidized housing on the top floor of 700 Ontario Street, a large apartment building in the area now known as Saint James Town. Half the residents, it seemed to me, were poor people on welfare or stuck in minimum wage jobs. The other half were students who lacked money but anticipated interesting, prosperous futures for themselves and the families they would have one day.

To get to our apartment we took the elevator with its steel walls scratched with graffiti and floor stinking of urine. But our home had large windows overlooking the city and the lake. It was a splendid view. We had a bedroom, a study, and a bathroom. We felt fortunate to live in such modern accommodations. If only the bedbugs would stop marching boldly across the threshold, under the door, in broad daylight! Those bedbugs had no fear. At night, when we flipped on the bedroom light, swarms of them would vanish from their stations on the walls, only to reappear once we went back to sleep. Our bodies were covered with telltale red bumps. Fumigation was routine, both for the bedbugs and for the persistent cockroaches in the kitchen.

Those were dark days for me. I had no idea why I couldn't move forward, as my friends were doing, into careers of their choice. All I knew was I couldn't function in the adult world and was desperate for some way of relaxing the spasms in my shoulder, neck, and back muscles. I needed to quiet my mind and become more comfortable in my own skin.

I was drawn to yoga, with its promise of inner calm, like a starving woman to a banquet table.

It's curious, however, that I was drawn to yoga. In the sixties and seventies most North Americans associated yoga with culturally dissonant bodily contortions performed by skinny men in loincloths. I knew no one who practised yoga.

My relationship with yoga began when a paperback book jumped out at me from a shelf in the bookstore. I took my new guide back to our apartment and immediately began to practise the breathing exercises and the stretches. I longed to go to an actual yoga class, but that was too scary. What would I encounter? Incense and chanting? Fanatical people with hypnotic eyes? My imagination kept me from investigating the yoga classes advertised on a sign in a second-floor window on Bloor Street not far from where we lived. I never did find the courage to climb the stairs to investigate.

Some years later, though, after the birth of our son, Frank, and our move to an upper duplex on Mount Pleasant Rd., I actually found a yoga class. As luck would have it, Mooredale House, our local community centre, offered classes. There was no risk of running into an embarrassing situation in this respectable setting.

When I turned up for my first class in the coach house of Mooredale House, a small, energetic woman with short white hair introduced herself as our teacher. This was Adelinde Ostermann, a former German army nurse who was now a devotee of yoga's healing power. From the first class I was hooked. Never before had I enjoyed physical exercise. I was fascinated with my body's response to the postures or asanas. In a yoga class, in my mat space on the floor, it was safe to feel what was happening in my body. As the months went by my muscles firmed up. I felt more energetic and even peaceful for hours at a time.

When Adelinde asked me if I was interested in training with her to become a yoga teacher I jumped at the opportunity. (At that time there was no formal training.) I imagined being a yoga teacher. Yoga teachers are calm and wise. I would be calm and wise! I would reinvent myself. I would work so hard on myself that I would completely change my timid, scared being into a confident, wise yoga teacher.

Of course when I actually began teaching sections of the class as part of my apprenticeship I was a nervous wreck. Later, when I had my own classes, I managed my anxiety by asking students to lie down on their mats as soon as they entered the classroom. That way nobody would be looking at me until I calmed down. On weekends we yoga teachers often met at Adelinde's house for training sessions. Adelinde had one of those long, narrow four-plexes that line the streets near the lake in the Beaches area of Toronto. From her old-fashioned kitchen she served us *roggenbrot* (rye bread) and cottage cheese with an ever-present bowl of fresh fruit. A dozen of us early yoga teachers would sit on cushions on the floor of her living room in self-conscious lotus postures until our Western bodies shrieked with pain. We were determined to be real yogis.

One day Adelinde announced she had invited an actual swami to teach us. Much to my surprise Swami Sivananda Radha not only was a woman but a Westerner. Swami Radha, with her white, white hair and her warm brown eyes, took her place stretched out in a lawn chair at one end of the living room and invited us to open ourselves to her teaching.

For Swami Radha yoga was meant for self-examination. That first weekend I spent with her and the other yoga teachers at Adelinde's home, she led us through The Straight Walk workshop.

In the first part of our training in this Buddhist path to self-knowledge we each approached a table piled high with a wide variety of objects, ranging from a delicate brooch to a banana to a photo of a child. There must have been a hundred objects. We were directed in exactly how we should approach the table from different directions. Then we went off to write down all we could remember and ponder what we associated with the objects, what each item reminded us of. Naturally, the items you couldn't remember became the object of close examination. What in your life caused you to overlook the picture of the bearded man? Or the ornate brooch?

In the second part each of us was given a certain area to walk in, back and forth slowly, paying close attention to the feet, staying in the moment. It sounds simple, I know. But for most of us, walking like that for half an hour with no interruptions and no breaks severely challenged our mindfulness. I was given a hallway to walk in. By the end of my walk I had a profound new appreciation for what I valued in life and what was superficial.

Meeting Swami Sivananda Radha was a turning point for me. She had life experience. She knew what it was to be married and run a home. Here was a yogi who could understand my life. Unlike the teachers I was training with, she didn't think vegetarianism was the essence of yoga. Respect all food, she told us, not just the animals. Plants have feelings, too. All plants and animals are eaten by a higher species. Whatever you eat, do so in a spirit of reverence for the life that was sacrificed to nourish a higher species.

Swami Radha had been christened Sylvia Hellman. Born into an affluent German family, she shocked her proper social circle by becoming a performer and dancing professionally in German theatrical shows. Following the Second World War, having lost her husband and her property to the Nazis, she immigrated to Canada. As she told it, the great saint, Swami Sivananda of Rishikesh, India, appeared to her in a vision and urged her to come to India to study with him. In India he initiated her as a swami and sent her back to Canada with instructions to teach the eight paths of yoga and Eastern philosophy and psychology.

"Don't try to turn North Americans into Indian Hindus," he instructed her. "You have to find ways to adapt the teachings of the East for the West."

When I met her she had been teaching in Canada long enough to establish a yoga ashram in the mountains of British Columbia.

At the end of the weekend Swami Radha expressed an interest in spending time with me. We could walk along Queen Street, do some window shopping, and maybe go into a café for a coffee, she suggested. I was happy with her invitation and the next day we strolled along together, the swami and her starry-eyed student. I learned that Swami Radha was just coming off thirteen years of *tapas*, an extreme form of material renunciation and physical and spiritual self-discipline. During that time this beautiful woman had never bought clothes for herself. She relied on the bales of clothes sent as charity to her ashram. On her dancer's feet she had worn men's work boots. She had denied herself anything that didn't arrive in the cast-off barrel. Almost all of the donated clothing was for men. She'd felt the sting of the *tapas*. It was to last for twelve years but she voluntarily extended it for an extra year, to make sure she had broken her need for attractive clothing and material objects. In her pre-war life in Germany, she told me, no glass or candy dish was acceptable if it wasn't crystal. Only the finest fabrics and fashions would do.

Walking along the street she wandered in and out of the shops, indulging herself in fingering silk scarves and lace-trimmed blouses. Clearly she was delighting her senses with feminine colours and fabrics. Her long period of *tapas* was over. She could once more give into her appreciation of pretty colours and soft materials. Her delight surprised me and stirred my caring for this very human woman.

She was the most interesting woman I had ever met. And she was becoming my spiritual teacher, introducing me to a whole new way of being in the world. Swami Radha didn't share my poor opinion of myself. From our first meeting she took a special interest in me. She thought I was an old soul and I had only to break through my fears to become enlightened.

She regarded me with love and respect. Somehow she saw in me wisdom and the potential for helping others. When she looked at me, she said, she saw the most extraordinary light all around me.

I wrote in my journal:

Sunday, Oct. 24, 1976
Swami Radha told me she has never seen anyone with as much Light as I have. She tells me it radiates all around me very brilliantly and beautifully. Is this why I am able to give as a yoga teacher, even when I feel shaky? Do others see my Light?

I remember Swami Radha's words in an early letter. "Mary, you are very precious."

Am I destined for a Special Path? I find it exciting to think I am. Is it a sign of my life's purpose? It feels right!

What are the consequences of being "special" in this way? Loss of ego—I can't claim ownership of this power. I can only be a channel. Greater confidence—I have the "grace" to help others, to teach, to share.

One day she looked intently at me with her brown eyes and said, "Mary, you can have whatever wealth or material possessions come your way, as long as you use your good fortune to help others."

Being married to Harvey, I realized, was part of my dharma, my path. By now he had trained as a psychiatrist and was earning enough money to allow me to stay home with Frank. That left me with time and energy to study all I could with Swami Radha. She was a keen teacher. We spent hundreds of hours together in my kitchen or at the dining room table while she instructed me on the life of a yogi. When she wasn't in Toronto we carried on what amounted to a correspondence course. I sent her my writings and she replied with her thought-provoking questions and comments.

She was an early advocate of women's liberation. "You must develop your own areas of competence," she would say. "Don't let Harvey overpower you. Don't let him drag you down. It's your place to lift him up to your level and show him a more enlightened way of being."

"Mary," she told me in one piece of correspondence, "the marketplace and the temple are both sacred. Don't separate your life into 'ordinary' and 'holy.' All life is holy. Make your work in preparing a meal an act of prayer."

In another she wrote: "I know very few women who can maintain an attitude of prayer while doing housework. You'd have to tackle the dust in the corners imagining it to be the dust on your soul as you clean your inner space. I don't think you can do that. Women need a room of their own. Very few women, even those in a large house, have a room where they can close the door and leave everything untouched until they return. If you can't have a room, at least have part of a room which is out of bounds to others."

This led to some conflict between Harvey and me. He liked sharing a study with me. Nevertheless, since my days with Swami Radha, I have always valued having my own room for writing and meditating.

She wrote me to "make a special place in your house for prayer and meditation, even if it's just a place where you don't ordinarily sit."

On abortion: "It is hard to find a human birth. Usually the soul does not enter the fetus until the last moment. If a fetus is aborted, the soul is not destroyed. It simply goes looking for another birth."

On energy: "Think of your energy like fuel in your gas tank. Never run on your reserve."

More on energy: "Think of your energy as a bank account. Some activities and some people give you energy. These are like deposits into your account. Other activities or people drain you. These are withdrawals. Try to keep as much money in the bank as possible."

On food: "If you think it's bad for you, for goodness' sake, don't eat it."

When I first became serious about yoga Harvey was upset. It was one thing to go to a stretch class but I was beginning to talk about "spiritual" matters. He felt betrayed and embarrassed. Where was the sensible agnostic female he had married?

He also had mixed feelings about Swami Radha. He found her charming and interesting. He soon decided she wasn't crazy and that maybe she did know something to which the rest of us were blind. Half pleased and half worried, he used to say, "I get the feeling she sees you as her successor." He did not fully understand what this would mean. To follow in her footsteps, to be a swami, meant renouncing one's attachment to partners and children. Sexual energy and the energy that goes into close relationships were to be sublimated for use in serving others.

This period marked the beginning of a decade of close personal instruction with her. And it marked the beginning of important years of healing from my childhood wounding, which was still a mystery to me. I promised her to "take time to be holy" every day. This meant setting aside time for contemplation, journal writing, working on some aspect of myself she suggested needed attention, observing myself as I worked, noting my attitude as I gave service to others, and looking at everything in my life as a challenge that would aid in the expansion of my awareness.

Indeed as the years went by my spiritual teacher came up with ingenious ways to help me deal with practical issues in my life. For example, caring for Harvey's aging mother fell largely on me when we moved her into an apartment not far from where we lived.

By that time I had graduated in social work and set up a private practice, and Frank was in his final years of grade school. Meanwhile it was my job to take my mother-in-law to medical appointments, the bank, and shopping. Frank dropped in on her each day after school and went across the street to the grocery store for her everyday needs. He found her tales of the old days interesting. The two of them got along fine. As for me I really resented the way she never thanked me. I was embarrassed publicly by her tiresome attempts to be cute and funny with bank clerks and grocery store cashiers. She referred to herself as "the old battleaxe" and the title fit.

I presented my dilemma to Swami Radha. Looking after my mother-in-law was disturbing my wish to relate with love and compassion to all persons in my world, I told her. Mean and angry thoughts were interrupting my inner peace.

"You need to learn about selfless service," she said.

"Selfless service?"

"Yes, service where you expect nothing in return. You have to do it with no expectation of thanks or rewards."

"I don't know that I can do that. I'm no saint, you know."

"You'll be doing it for yourself. You're going to learn a lot about yourself by dealing with your mother-in-law this way. You'll be watching your behaviour and your thoughts each time you're with her. What is it that makes you angry? Is it your ego? This is a wonderful opportunity for your spiritual advancement."

During the next few years I cared for Harvey's mother with all the attention I would have given a project that was dear to my heart. The resentment drained out of the situation. I no longer felt impatient with her geriatric dawdling. I was strengthening my spiritual muscles, moving closer to enlightenment.

Swami Radha brought order into my chaos. I began each day by determining the priorities for that day. Everything else could fall into place around the most important events. Balance was central to the yogi's life. Balance, though, did not have to occur in the space of each day. It could be over a period of time. For example, on some days, getting things done may be the priority. On others, relaxing and self-care may be central themes.

Every day was marked with an earnest search for impeccable morality. What were my motives in helping someone? Did I expect a reward? What was the effect on others of any action I took? Why did I lie? (Not *did* I lie?)

Swami Radha gave few specific instructions regarding my spiritual practices. Her one order was, "Twice a day sit quietly in a place you choose in your home. Some place where you don't ordinarily sit. Quiet your mind, watch your breathing, then do your mantra practice."

A mantra is a word or group of words you repeat to yourself in order to keep a part of your mind in the present when it would otherwise be drawn to ruminating and worrying, to fears about the future or shame about the past. The yogi stays in the here and now by repeating the mantra over and over and over in her mind. The mantra may be given to you by a spiritual teacher (a *guru mantra*) or it may be one that you choose (an *ishta mantra*). Whichever it is, once you receive it, you must not change it. This is part of the discipline. You will no doubt begin to think that another mantra would serve you better. If you wish to follow the tradition of the mantra, you need to resist this temptation to change.

Journal writing, self-observation, and dream study were part of the discipline. Each day I was to write in my journal and not just when I felt depressed or troubled. By writing every day I could observe Swami Radha's teaching that life is a wave. Moods change. Emotions fluctuate. She was training me to realize that *I* was not my emotions. By reading about the good days when I was upset, I had the experience of knowing my mood would change again and I'd feel like a different person. "You are not your body, you are not your emotions, you are Light!" Swami Radha would remind me.

When I pushed past my fatigue to practise yoga I found release for some of the tautness in my muscles. I also got relief from the feelings of fear coursing through my gut day and night. If I just did enough yoga, I reasoned, maybe I could lead a more normal life. The breathing and the asanas (exercises) never failed to bring me a sense of peace, different from the deadness to which I had become accustomed.

I slowly started to like myself better. I began to feel I was a good person. I was also doing something that greatly benefited others. My success and skill at teaching yoga shone back at me from the loving faces of my students. They told me how their classes with me enabled them to be more patient with their children, more loving in the world, or less tense at work. Sometimes I couldn't help but be hard on myself for not being able to achieve with yoga in my own life what my students seemed to manage in theirs. At other times I'd laugh to myself about how I was probably the world's most nervous yoga teacher. More and more, though, I was actually finding I was wise and incredibly attuned to my students. As I walked around the carpeted room where the students were lying or sitting on the floor, I would intuitively move to the asana that was needed by reading someone's stiff shoulders or tight lower back. Each student felt the class was just for her.

Nothing helps build self-esteem like success.

With the asanas something was happening that I did not understand at the time. My own young body was becoming fit. It actually belonged to me for the first time in my life. I was able to like my body and feel comfortable in it. I was happy with its sleek muscles and trim shape. This was a time when adults did not exercise much. My yoga classes attracted people like me who enjoyed the gentleness and relaxation of yoga but would never have gone to a gym. There were few aerobics or keep-fit classes in those days. Like me, many got turned onto exercise through yoga.

The strong connection with Swami Radha was all-important. Yoga is an ancient discipline. At that time, even before it became popular in the West, people around the world practised the same asanas and read the same scriptures. By becoming Swami Radha's disciple I joined a cosmos of universal consciousness, saints, gurus, and yogis.

A disciple is the guru's student, but much, much more. In the East it is spoken of as a marriage. In karmic terms, once the guru-disciple relationship is established, it lasts many lifetimes. The guru accepts the responsibility for directing the disciple towards enlightenment. The disciple, for her part, accepts the guru's impenetrable wisdom and her understanding of a reality that is beyond the reach of most humans.

Discipline, love for oneself and for others, staying in the present moment by concentrating on the breath and the body— all of this was part of yoga training. I'd never heard the term "affect regulation," the buzz phrase for the psychological healing of trauma victims, but that's what I got thanks to yoga and Swami Radha. She taught me to breathe in ways that calmed my panicking mind—ways that settled the electrical surges of fear in my body.

I taught yoga and gave workshops in related topics for a dozen years. Swami Radha's approach was largely psychological. Students practised yoga postures for her, learning about themselves. What do you think about as you do a shoulder stand or plough? How does the fact that it is hard to speak in these postures affect you? If you found it hard to bend forward, where in life do you have trouble bending or being flexible? Everything yoga teaches is about knowing yourself. Know thyself and be free. That's what it's all about, said Swami Radha. The evolution of consciousness is everything.

Yoga asanas helped me stay in the present. All the asanas are about mindfulness. The mind is constantly alert to the subtle changes in the body. In a yoga asana, whether standing or sitting or lying down, we ask ourselves: What part of me is resisting this stretch? Am I able to go farther? Or is this as far as I can stretch without injuring myself? What needs to happen (mentally and physically) for me to reach my potential in this posture? We want to challenge our body, to take it to its physical edge, while respecting its limitations.

Being present is the opposite of *dissociating*. If we can practise being present we can reverse the habit of automatically dissociating whenever we are stressed emotionally. I aspired to stay present all day, every day.

Another way to practise staying in the present is to adapt the practice of mindfulness meditation in your daily life. Suppose you have carrots to peel for supper. How much more interesting to stay fully concentrated, saying to yourself, "Peeling carrots, peeling carrots, mind wandering, peeling carrots, running water, rinsing carrots."

These were heady years. I was involved in a search for the ultimate truth, an unveiling of the secrets of the universe, an impeccable morality. The search offered certainty and the expectation that, if I worked hard enough, I would one day arrive "there." "There" was a state of enlightenment, attainable by those who followed the guru's teachings. After I had spent years as an earnest seeker after truth, Swami Radha would encourage me by telling me that I was almost "there."

The excitement of learning to live *consciously* was not the only bonus of my new, fulfilling life. Some of my yoga students became interested in yoga beyond the physical exercises and joined me in studying Swami Radha's teachings. Over time they became peers and close friends. Together we lovingly supported one another in our lives and in our studies. My lonely days were over. I had never felt so connected and so cared for.

In Toronto during the seventies, when Frank was a little boy, I was Swami Radha's representative, so to speak. Besides my yoga classes I ran a weekly dream study group and gave workshops based on the guru's teachings. For me it was an idyllic period of meaningful work and spiritual companionship. Everyone who was interested was welcomed to our groups. We shared the excitement and sense of purpose of being involved in something of the utmost importance.

Looking back I smile over the way we struggled to interpret the most offhand remark by Swami Radha as a statement of profound wisdom. Whatever she said on her frequent visits to our Toronto group we mined for a deeper meaning. In retrospect I realize that the philosophical interpretations we came up with often were products of our need for an all-wise leader. Sometimes our guru was just an ordinary person making mundane comments about the world.

During my decade as Swami Radha's disciple I organized workshops for her, usually hosting them in my home. My yoga students and anyone else who wanted to learn from this remarkable woman were welcome. She moved into our guest bedroom for a week at a time. For the most part her visits to our house twice a year worked out well. She was a thoughtful visitor and always cleaned up after herself. Occasionally, when there would be too many phone calls for her or too many visitors wanting to pay their respects, Harvey would grumble that entertaining Swami Radha was like hosting the bishop.

One weekend especially stands out in my mind. I was hosting a workshop for Swami Radha. Harvey was supposed to be away until Sunday night, but his plans changed. The workshop started Friday evening. He wasn't too happy about people chanting mantras in our rec room. He sniped that he had thought it was a "workshop" and at workshops he was familiar with people worked and talked. They didn't sit on the floor making bizarre sounds that made no sense.

Saturday afternoon he went off on his bicycle to play squash. He called me a couple of hours later, right in the middle of the workshop. He had hurt his back and was in great pain. In fact he could barely move. He wanted me to jump in the car right away and bring him home. I headed for the squash courts filled with a mixture of concern for his injury and resentment at being pulled away from my guru's teachings. One part of me was sure he'd hurt himself just to interfere with my spiritual pursuits.

When I brought him home I settled him into the black leather La-Z-Boy in his study and returned to the incredible teachings taking place in our rec room.

At five the workshop ended for the day. We would meet the next day, Sunday, at ten in the morning. There was a knock at our front door. When I opened it the great spiritual leader Swami Venkatesananda swept in, followed by his entourage of unusual-looking people. He had heard Swami Radha was in town and had come to visit her. She was delighted to see him. Everyone was very excited. Orange robes fluttered about around the house as someone used the bathroom or got a glass of water from the kitchen. I was so caught up in the honour and privilege of having the great Venkatesananda in my home that I completely forgot about Harvey.

When my eyes finally sought him out he was still lying there, unable to move, in his black La-Z-Boy. From his study he could watch the whole performance. His face was the face of a helpless man undergoing torture.

I could only conclude that the powers of spiritual leaders, like beauty, are in the eye of the beholder. A funny-looking guy with a shaved head who is wrapped in bright orange robes can bring thousands to their knees in reverence and prayer. For others he has no authority and is merely a dissonant intrusion.

As the years went on yoga became more and more central to my life. It was my work, my relaxation, my most meaningful social connection with other aspirants, and my way of feeling comfortable in my body. Swami Radha urged me to come to her ashram in Kootenay Bay, B.C. It was very important for me to be there with her, to learn more, to get closer to "there," to enlightenment. I was getting very close, she once again assured me.

I wrote in my journal:

Sunday evening, May 23, 1976
Swami Radha and I talk. She tells me how I could be the head of a yoga centre, take a real role in life, end the feeling of being Number Two in my marriage. We talk about money and Harvey's attitude to money as well as my own. To do this, however, I would have to take the Teachers Course at the ashram.

At first this was unthinkable. I couldn't possibly leave Harvey for that long. (It never occurred to me to leave seven-year-old

Frank at home. She had assured me Frank would be welcome and would have a good experience there.) I approached Harvey with my thoughts. In fact, with Swami Radha's support, I told him I was going, with or without him. He decided to come. A cold winter at home with no family did not appeal to him.

So in 1976, right after Christmas, the three of us set out to drive across the country in our little brown Mazda. We were wedged in so tightly that we realized, after the first few hundred miles, there was no way we could switch drivers as planned. Our belongings stuffed us into our positions. Harvey was the driver and I was in the passenger seat. Frank had just enough space in the back seat to fit his small body beside a tightly packed pile of our worldly goods.

We drove north to Sault Ste. Marie, across the top of Lake Superior, and then on to the Prairies. Our nights were spent in motels along the way where our son complained he couldn't possibly sleep with the lights on and the two of us talking.

He was much more positive about visiting every possible hot spring along the way. As soon as we reached Alberta there were many of these wonders of nature—hot water bubbling up in steaming pools, creating a cover of mist in the freezing landscapes where mountain sheep cavorted in the steep hills surrounding Banff Upper Hot Springs. In B.C. we found Radium Hot Springs and Ainsworth Hot Springs. I remember one dark winter night under a full moon I swam through the steamy water in search of Frank and Harvey. I popped up out of the darkness to give them a cheery greeting, only to discover, to my embarrassment, that the smaller blond head belonged to a woman embracing her man.

We finally reached the Yashodhara Ashram, which is nestled in the Kootenay Valley in southeast British Columbia, not far from the town of Nelson. On the day we arrived heavy snowfall loaded the branches of the trees. I ran out with my camera to capture the beauty of the scene but I needn't have hurried. The snow stayed for weeks, never to be blown away by any wind, such is the peace of the valley. Kootenay Lake lies at the bottom of the steeply sloping land. The log guesthouse overlooks the bookstore and office, dining hall, and prayer room, which are strung out in that order down the side of the mountain to the lake. Swami Radha's house, Many Mansions, was also positioned to look out over the lake. It lay beyond the vegetable gardens, the farm building, and the print shop that published the Swami's writings.

Once the three of us settled into our room in the guest house, all was not peaceful. Harvey decided this was not a place he could tolerate for three months. In his view the residents and teachers were living some sort of delusion. They did not know how to separate proven fact from merely interesting ideas. They placed equal value on science and unproven theories. He felt like going back to Toronto.

I said he could go (which would probably have meant the end of our marriage). He said that if he went he expected to take Frank with him. I refused. Frank was staying with me in this loving environment. As it turned out Harvey changed his mind and settled in for the three months, even participating wholeheartedly in the program.

A typical day at the ashram started early with a hatha yoga class, followed by breakfast in the main dining room. The rest of the day was spent in classes and workshops until suppertime.

Workshops varied from the study of the scripture of the Bhagavad Gita and the Sutras to exercises designed to sharpen our five senses. What smell is coming from this bottle? What happens if you stare at a blue dot? Can you become very still inside and listen to whatever sounds come into your awareness?

Slowly and thoughtfully chew a piece of apple, a piece of banana, a section of orange.

In some classes we experimented with sound. "Om" is the universal sound. Feel how the "a," "u," and "m" vibrate in your body. Chanting brought on a natural high. Dream study, the Tibetan approach to interpreting dreams, was central to our intensive training. At the end of classes, after supper, we would go farther down the hill to the prayer room. There we took turns leading *satsang*, the worship practised by yogis. Wrapped in gray blankets we sat cross-legged on the floor looking out over Kootenay Lake as the leader for that night played the harmonium, an enchanting instrument whose keyboard and bellows blend magically with the human voice. The leader chose the mantra for chanting, the readings, and the prayers. Anyone could lead a *satsang*. All have equal access to a Higher Power.

Satsang was not the end of the day. Once we returned to the log guesthouse at the top of the mountain we still had at least one paper to prepare for the next day. Following a quick check-in with Frank about his day Harvey and I would position ourselves at our desks to type the required papers. Usually the papers were based on the day's workshop, urging us to form our personal reactions to scriptures, Buddhist psychology, or sensory experiments. Time off was rare. A free day presented endless possibilities for taking care of personal needs.

As a student at the ashram I began to have a different perception of my beloved Swami. She who was the charming, thoughtful guest had another side. At Yashodhara she was the boss. People were actually afraid of her. Her young swami, Swami Sivananda, named after her own guru, was often set up for public humiliation, even though he was one of our main teachers. His humble, apologetic responses to Swami Radha were evidently meant to teach us that she was the ultimate authority.

As for me I squirmed for him and questioned her wish to shame him publicly.

She lived in her delightful, airy Many Mansions with its collection of orchids, surrounded by young devotees who gathered around her in the evenings to soak in the wisdom of her words. Men and women embroidered spiritual pictures as they listened, using coloured thread and crude patterns stencilled in blue on white cloth. I thought about how my old mother would have enjoyed the attention of this circle of intelligent young adults—though, granted, she would have offered them Johnnie Walker, not sewing needles.

On the occasions that Swami Radha appeared to give a lecture we were all to be appropriately in a state of reverent awe. No one talked casually with her or—heaven forbid—joked with her. Where had my lovely Swami gone?

Harvey referred to her as the Hohenzollern princess and I couldn't help but laugh. Nobody else dared to be anything but respectful and in awe, it seemed.

I had the strange experience of living in a closed system. The culture in which you live defines what life is. The rest of the world, the world beyond the mountain valley, was far away. There was no radio, no television, no newspaper. All of this was deliberate. You were here for three precious months and nothing must pull you from all there was to learn. You needed your concentration for all the workshops and classes. You needed to cleanse your mind of worldly distractions.

The result was that the rule of the Swami took on dimensions unimaginable in the wider world. There was nothing to offset her power. She bestowed kindness when she felt like it and harshness where she observed imperfect loyalty to her teachings.

Still, there was much to be gained from the ashram's intensive program. I remember a period when Harvey was so fascinated with dream interpretation it seemed he was awake beside me in the bed half the night, flashlight shining on the page as he recorded yet another dream. To my great relief our teacher told us we didn't need to remember every dream every night since all our dreams in a particular period would likely deal with whatever issue was current for us.

At the end of our three months there we were all thriving. Harvey was grateful for his new appreciation of something beyond the concrete world of science. In fact he became a mystic, aware of all that we do not know about our world. Soon after we left the ashram he began to write a paper, "One Physician's Experience with Yoga," which described his time at Yashodhara Ashram. Published in the *Canadian Medical Association Journal*, his paper described to Western physicians just what yoga is about. He also expressed his appreciation for the maturity of our teachers. The paper drew a huge response from readers requesting copies.

Frank was full of confidence after his three months at the mountain school with the ashram residents. As for me, I had expanded my awareness and felt truly confident as a yoga teacher.

It was the beginning of April when we climbed into the car to return home. Spring was coming to the gentle land of the ashram. Small green shoots were appearing on the southern slope of the mountain. Patches of green were showing through the snow. It was time to go back to Toronto.

I will never forget the first morning in our own home. The three of us sat in the dining room. The space and privacy were wonderful. I recognized how I valued *my* house, *my* kitchen, *my* dining room. I was no renunciant. Any thoughts of becoming a spiritual aspirant with no loved ones of my own, no house to call mine, and no right to privacy were finally put to rest.

The demanding course gave me the courage to go back to school. I had withstood the rigours of nightly papers and felt confident in my ability to meet the requirements of the course. By the next September I had applied for and been accepted into the University of Toronto's two-year master's program in social work.

Why did I choose social work? In my role as a yoga teacher I found I was good at the ad hoc counselling that took place with my students before and after class. As well I sometimes worked with students who were terminally ill. Palliative care, which deals with death and dying, was a new area for our society to tackle. The School of Social Work beckoned. There I could earn a master's degree in two years, with summers off.

The next step on my journey was under way.

Chapter 7

Frankie

Frankie, as we called him then, was born one snowy January night in 1969 when Harvey and I had been married for seven years.

Being pregnant joined me to all the mysterious cycles of nature. For the first time I had a deep bond with the females in my world. I belonged among women and I belonged in the universe, with all its miracles of creation. I witnessed the changes happening in my body with all the wonder of Eve on the first day of creation. I was taking part in the marvel of procreation!

Just after Frank was born he lay in my arms, totally relaxed, breathing from deep down in his tiny belly. His newborn hair was long and black. With his dark hair and blue identification beads around his wrist, the nurses named him The Hippy. Once home I spent hours just witnessing the wonder of his yawns and sneezes. He and I were one being. When he drooled I drooled. Spooning baby food into his mouth, I smacked my own lips.

The duplex where we lived had two bedrooms. One was Harvey's and mine. The other was Harvey's study, which now doubled as a nursery. The arrangement was fine until Frank grew old enough to pull himself up on the bars of his crib. Then he'd stand there, bouncing excitedly, reaching out to Dadda. Dadda wasn't getting much studying done and Frankie wasn't developing good sleep habits.

I found us a three bedroom house with a backyard and a basement. Frank could have his own room and Harvey could study undisturbed. By this time Harvey was a resident in psychiatry, having chosen a branch of medicine that would allow him a decent home life.

Our red brick house backed onto a spacious grassy yard with a pear tree. Harvey built a sandbox at the end of the garden where we sipped our after-dinner coffee under the boughs of the pear tree, all the while playing in the sand with Frankie. With a back porch off the kitchen, my little boy, and my yoga classes, I was actually happy a lot of the time. It is a period of warm memories.

Harvey was also enchanted by our baby. He loved to hold tiny Frank in his huge hands, playing baby games of blowing into his face and gently teasing him with his soother. When my mother came to visit she looked on at this father-child play with disgust. The sight of muscular arms cuddling Frank's small body drew her disapproval. Men were not supposed to be interested in babies. There was something indecent about a man caring for a baby.

Sometimes our joy knew no bounds. The future belonged to us and to our little guy. It was a time of loving and laughing.

It was also a time of terrible fights. On many occasions savage rage flared up between us. The usual issues that lit the kindling of our underlying resentments were my "incompetence" and Harvey's long hours at work. I just couldn't do anything right. I'd always forget to do whatever Harvey asked of me. Looking back I realize I was filled with anger I had no way to express. My anger came out in ways that frustrated Harvey. As well my head was often fogged over, causing me to be absent-minded. By the time we finished tearing strips off each other's souls we would inevitably begin raging about each other's mothers. It was a no-holds-barred battle of words. We knew each other's tender spots.

Then one day during an ugly fight we noticed our little boy sitting in the cold ashes in the fireplace. He was dressed for bed in his turquoise sleepers and now was padding around the room trailing ashes across the living room floor. Oh my god. What were we doing to him?

"Oh, Frank!" We snatched him up, ashes and all. "Mommy and Daddy are really silly for fighting. We're sorry, sweetheart."

Our shame cut deep. How could we drive such a sweet little guy to be the sacrificial lamb, desperate for a way to stop the adults from fighting?

Some of our best times in those early days were spent on the island property we bought in Georgian Bay when Frank was two. Starting with an umbrella tent by the water we spent the summers getting to know the fish life, the mink that ran across our rocky shore, and the otter couple who played nearby. The umbrella tent gave way to a palatial tent in the woods, complete with a cook shelter and zip-open windows. In the evening as Harvey and I played Scrabble in the cook shelter by the light of a Coleman lamp, flying squirrels perched on our shoulders. We had become part of the woodland life and the other creatures were fearless. If Frankie had had an afternoon sleep we got him up to watch the eleven o'clock mice when they came to feast on the unwashed dinner dishes.

Over the years we built a cabin to shelter us from the weather. It was sixteen feet by sixteen feet because the lumber came in eight-foot lengths. We had no electrical power and were unwilling to change the dimensions sawing by hand. Each change to the property brought greater comfort as well as a loss of closeness to nature. Once we had indoor plumbing we no longer saw much of the stars at night. We lost our contact with the woodland creatures. The trade-off was shelter from the elements, real beds, and a cabin we could lock up when we returned to the city. It was the evolution of mankind experienced by a man, a woman, and a little boy.

Frank's friendship with Swami Radha began when he was four. Often she told him stories, sometimes with her fingers. In these stories her fingers magically acted out characters that would come alive. In one our dining room table became the forest where young deer bounded about as a buck and a doe whispered with parental pride about their young one.

When Frank was in junior and senior kindergarten he often awoke with dreams of The Purple Lady. These were special dreams where he felt very loved and happy. He often talked about The Purple Lady—until he was too old to confide such tender happenings. Since Swami Radha, when she wasn't in orange robes, usually wore purple, I wondered about these dreams. Was he having mystical experiences? Was he space travelling? I never knew for sure how magical she was.

Frank also reported several times that Swami Radha, who lived in British Columbia, had been at his school that day. I would ask him what she was doing there. He thought she was there to teach French to the big kids. Who knows what really happened? Certainly not I.

The winter Harvey and I spent at the ashram, Frank was one of half a dozen children who were living there with their parents.

Lynette Halldorson, a disciple of Swami Radha, was in charge of the children after school. She was warm and attuned to the children. Her cookie-baking and her creative recreation with them were rich and loving. Each morning Lynette escorted the children up the long hill out of the ashram to the highway to catch the school bus to their mountain school. Her presence kept the children safe from the cougars, which were known to attack small children who were unaccompanied by adults.

The two-room schoolhouse for the younger children was nestled into the side of a mountain. Ashram children were warmly welcomed by the young female teacher. At first Frank was discouraged because in this new grade two, you had to spell words like "cougar," "glacier," and "avalanche." By the time he left, his spelling skills, as well as his reading and mathematical skills, had greatly improved.

I felt the loss of closeness with my child. By choice Frank ate with the rest of the children and with his ashram friends. I remember feeling frantic that I was not supervising exactly what went into his mouth at meals. Was he getting enough protein? Was he drinking his milk? It was hard to let go of my control and trust the healthy ashram meals and the other adults who were encouraging him to eat well. I have to say, he was wonderfully healthy and energetic. There was certainly no sign of inadequate nurturing, either physical or emotional.

In the evenings Frank's parents were busy tapping out the required paper for the next day's classes on two electric typewriters. After the first few nights with all three of us in the same room nothing could keep him awake—not the constant stream of visitors coming by our room, not the clacking of the typewriters, and not the frequent red wine parties.

Frank has fond memories of his time at the ashram where he was one of a group of children who went to the hen house to collect the eggs for the next day. He developed a personal relationship with Carolyn, the Holstein milk cow. He celebrated his eighth birthday at the ashram and was allowed to choose the menu for the dinner, as well as his birthday cake. He could invite a friend from school. He chose his friend Lewis.

"Tell me about Lewis," I prompted. "Why is he so nice to be with?"

Frank started to laugh. "Oh, Mom, you can't believe what we do at lunchtime. It's so funny."

More giggles. "I can't tell you." It was something really embarrassing.

Red flags went up. "What do you and Lewis do during the lunch hour?" I was preparing to deal with something sexual.

"We go behind the woodpile at the back of the school." More giggles. "Oh I can't tell you."

By now I was getting really worried.

"Tell me, Frank. What do you and Lewis do behind the woodpile? I really want to know."

There was more giggling, more claiming that it was too strange to tell me. I insisted.

"Oh, okay," he finally said. "We go behind the woodpile, get down on our knees, and say our prayers before eating our lunch."

"Oh," I said.

Chapter 8

Back to School

The ashram course gave me the courage to re-enter academia. That didn't mean I marched off confidently those first September mornings to the University of Toronto's School of Social Work. It was 1978. I was almost forty years old. The biggest library I'd been to in the past seventeen years was our friendly neighbourhood one, usually to take Frank to story hour or find him books in the children's section. The new Robarts Library with its up-to-date and complex technology and microfiche intimidated me. Its stunning architecture made me feel even smaller and more insignificant in the vast university setting.

I had graduated from my four-year honours undergraduate course in 1962, when the university didn't even have a computer. Now I was required to learn Fortran, a computer language, in order to put my data on cards that were then punched full of holes and fed into the computer. The computer filled a whole room, blocked off to students by a long, chest-high counter. Standing on the side of the counter away from the computer I would hand my cards to the expert who would then disappear and reappear with the printout I needed.

Frank was about to turn nine when I registered at the School of Social Work. I had made the decision to train in work that would prepare me to make a difference in some area of society that was neglected. There were so many unmet needs in the world. Death and dying was a brand-new field. Till then dying had been a taboo subject. Studies at the time noted that nurses spent far less time with the dying than with other patients. Nobody talked with people who were dying about what was happening to them. No one discussed their fears, wishes, or specific needs. They faced their final stage of life alone.

It was unexplored territory, a new discipline. In England Cecily Saunders was establishing hospice centres where the dying lived among caring, supportive health-care professionals. Thanks to accurate diagnoses of their pain and to medicine's painkillers the dying were more likely to be comfortable, able to think with clear minds and talk to their loved ones.

In Canada Dr. Balfour Mount started a palliative care program at the Royal Victoria Hospital in Montreal, Quebec. He himself had been very ill in a hospital and had personally witnessed the lack of empathy and compassion bestowed upon those patients who were not getting better. I decided I needed to learn from Dr. Mount. I wanted to be involved in this new, exciting area.

Ad hoc counselling had been part of the job in the years I was a yoga teacher. Before and after classes I often sat and listened to my female students struggle with issues such as their responsibilities, resentments, and guilt over their roles as wives and mothers. I liked this work and felt my ability to listen was helpful.

I had also worked with yoga students who were facing death. The recent works of Dr. Elisabeth Kübler-Ross, a pioneer in death and dying research and treatment, were my guide. However, in my capacity as a yoga teacher, I was not allowed to follow these students into the hospital, or if I was, nurses interrupted our sessions. I was there as a visitor, as a friend, with no professional recognition.

I wanted to be part of the care team. I wanted to be welcomed to the patient's bedside, not ushered away because I wasn't covered by the hospital's liability insurance.

I looked around for training that would allow me to learn counselling skills and work with the dying in hospitals as well as within the general population. I needed training in Western psychology to work with people who were not prepared to learn yoga. The master's program at the School of Social Work appealed to me. In two years I could learn how to assess and work with a wide population of people. The program included a practicum, an opportunity to work with clients under supervision.

In applying for admission to graduate school I was required to write a lengthy autobiography and discussion of life views and aspirations. The school wanted to know what I would do with my training. I knew the answer to this question. I had already written all over my applications that palliative care was the field in which I wanted to work.

In the fall of my first year I travelled to Montreal for a workshop with Dr. Balfour Mount, where I learned the newest information about treating the dying. Then I began a practicum at Toronto's Queen Elizabeth Hospital, where I was given a placement with a dying patient in the geriatric department. Throughout the early months I listened to my client compassionately and even went in over the Christmas holiday period to bring him comfort.

Much to my disappointment the physician in charge of the service to which I was assigned knew nothing of the new approaches in palliative care. He still ordered the nurses to withhold the next dose of morphine so the patient wouldn't become addicted. "Wouldn't become addicted?" I wanted to scream. "The poor man is dying!" In this doctor's care patients were still dying in pain, in spite of available information about preventing needless pain in someone's final days. My frustration was immense. I tried to interest him in what I had learned from Dr. Mount in Montreal, only to receive the equivalent of a dismissive pat on the head.

Forty seemed to be the cut-off age for admission to the master's program. A number of us had young children at home. During those first weeks when it was hard to keep track of each other's names we formed a cohort and simply called out "mommy" to each other in a shrill, small voice. It always worked. All of us were programmed to respond to that sound.

My stress level was sky-high in that first year. I'd been running a tight ship, both at home and as a yoga teacher. Now I felt like I knew nothing. I didn't understand many of the words being used around me. The environment was strange— and exciting. In those first classes I felt as if I was the only one who didn't feel at home. Most of my classmates were just out of undergraduate school.

The time came for the first assignment: General Systems Theory as applied to one's placement. I tackled the job with relish. How naive I was. I thought people at the School of Social Work, like Swami Radha and teachers at the ashram, would value my opinions. I didn't bother to include anything the professor would already know, assuming that she, too, had read the literature. When I picked up my paper from a pile outside her office door I saw a big F on the cover page. What did that mean? It wasn't my initial and it wasn't hers. Slowly, painfully, it dawned on me: F stood for failure. I couldn't believe it. I had asked Harvey to take on extra parenting duties so I could go to school. I was making life harder for Frank. Was it all for nothing? Had I made a big mistake?

In the end I swallowed my pride and went to the professor for help. She was generous with her time and encouragement. I knew that if I was going to succeed in this milieu I had to learn the ways of academia. After all I'd come here to learn new things. I did learn. I even came to appreciate the rigours of the scholarly paper. My next paper received an A.

At home Harvey took his turn as "lunch mother" at Frank's school and looked after him on holidays when I was at the university. Harvey had assured me he would support me in every way possible when I returned to school. It was my turn, he said. I'd been behind him during all his years of medical training. He didn't mind what we had for dinner as long as we spent time together over a meal.

And that's how it worked out. Frank learned to bake frozen pizza and Harvey made sure Frank got to his guitar lessons safely on the subway. On the mornings of the lesson, Harvey would take Frank's guitar to his office reception area. Come four o'clock, he could tell at a glance whether Frank had arrived to pick it up for his lesson, which was next door to Harvey's office.

However, nine-year-old Frank was not happy about what he saw as my abandonment of him. Before school started I had taken him down to Bloor Street to show him where I would be spending much of the next two years. He shoved his hands deep into his pockets, trudging along with his head down and his mouth pulled into a frown. When we passed Varsity Stadium I sought to cheer him up.

"Look, Frank, there's the stadium where they play all those football games," I said.

He barely looked at me as he said, "I guess you'll be going to a lot of football games and parties, eh Mom?"

So that was it. His image of university was learned from television. Somehow his mother was going to turn into one of those partying college students.

Just how unhappy he was became evident three weeks into my first semester, when he set fire to my frilly turquoise patio umbrella, a very feminine stand-in for his mother. It was the day when the cleaning woman came to our house, which meant Frank could come home for lunch. Out on the patio he'd been threatening the long, white fringe of the umbrella with the flame of the barbecue lighter. All at once the entire plastic umbrella burst into flames. He panicked. He was in real trouble now. Scared and in tears he phoned his father at the office. Instead of scolding him, Harvey sensed the underlying distress and told Frank he'd be right home.

As Harvey later told me, he pulled Frank close to him and let him know that his father understood how hard the changes were now that I was going to school. Harvey phoned the school to let them know that Frank wouldn't be there that afternoon. The two of them went off to buy Frank some new running shoes. To this day Frank talks about the day his father dropped everything at work to be with his troubled son.

As time went on I developed a comfortable routine. Weather permitting I rode my pink racer bicycle to school each day. Coming home I would stop in a park to review the day and get ready to re-enter my home where Frank was waiting. Of course I spent every night studying, writing papers, and generally living the life of a graduate student. Unlike my young class-mates I couldn't spend hours in the library. I bought a lot more books than they did and learned to make the most of my brief forays into the library. Sometimes I envied their freedom to just study and take care of themselves.

After my first year studying social work, summer holidays came early—as soon as exams were finished in May. I was free to ... to what? I didn't know. Instead of being free and happy I was restless, agitated, and depressed. Now that I had time to reflect I realized I no longer knew myself. Where had that organized yoga teacher gone? In the first week of classes the professors bluntly stated they were out to "socialize" us "to the profession." I remember shuddering at the thought of being socialized to anything. Was this the result? A stirred up, conflicted, moody woman who put off doing all the things she'd been looking forward to all year?

Weeks went by and I gradually became interested in running, tennis, and, of course, yoga. I was reconnecting with my physical self. Frank was happy that I joined him on school outings and started running on school mornings with him and a group of youngsters organized by the neighbourhood fathers. Harvey and I went out to movies and had friends over for dinner. All in all, by the time September rolled around again I had sorted myself out and was ready to return for another year.

I'd entered social work aspiring to work in the field of palliative care. By the time I graduated I was much less interested. After graduation friends still cut out articles and gave me books on death and dying. I looked at their offerings and thought, "Why are you giving this to me?" My interest had definitely waned. Perhaps it was because, in the past two years, palliative care had become more established as an area worthy of professional dedication. So many good people were taking up the cause. That made it less compelling for me. Perhaps it was because we become desensitized to anything, even death, if we immerse ourselves in it. Or perhaps I had done what I needed to do for myself: think about and work through my own inevitable death.

By the time I graduated I couldn't imagine myself working within the constraints of an agency, hospital, or institution. In any of these settings I would have to conform to the current model of practice. I knew there were so many ways I could help people—ways that mainstream services didn't recognize. Besides, people simply did not fit into theories and models. I knew, too, that we live life in our bodies. Without healing the body all the cognitive understanding in the world won't bring about real change. What was I going to do?

The universe helped me out. Robbers broke into our house one evening during the March break when I was in my second year at school and stole a silver tea set given to Harvey's parents for their wedding and another tea set presented to my grandfather on his retirement. (The price of silver was at an all-time high.) I got enough money from the insurance to renovate a space for my work in the nearby plaza. I outfitted a large carpeted room for yoga classes and a small office for my counselling practice.

The School of Social Work had given me good basic training, yet I knew there was so much more I could do as a therapist if only I could find a way to integrate the body's knowing with talk therapy.

When I opened my private practice I taught my yoga classes in the carpeted room and saw a few clients in my office as my counselling practice slowly grew. At the same time I was on the lookout for some way I could combine yoga's recognition of the body with Western psychology.

Meanwhile, I reconnected with Swami Radha, as I'd always intended to. My two years at school were meant merely as a hiatus in my life as her disciple. As soon as I set up my studio and office I arranged a weekend workshop for her. Back to the good old days—or so I thought.

Excited by the prospect of getting back the magic of the old days I invited my yoga students and anyone else I thought would benefit from Swami Radha's workshop. By seven o'clock on Friday evening, fifteen of us were assembled in my carpeted yoga room. I think the workshop was The Life Seal, in which participants draw, colour, and paste a visual collage of their strengths, weaknesses, hopes, and aspirations. One by one we would present bristol board images of our lives to Swami Radha for interpretation.

From the start of the workshop she seemed displeased with me. Her warmth and love for me were gone. At the noon hour on Saturday, when I returned from lunch later than she had, she was bristling with indignation. I'd left her standing outside my locked office door. She made it clear with her tight mouth and hard eyes that this was not acceptable.

We sat in a circle on floor cushions and chairs. Windows on one whole side of the room looked out onto a treed hillside. The sun dappled through into the room. I felt pleased with the tasteful setting and my new venture.

When it came time to present my Life Seal to Swami Radha I had no idea what was coming. I probably started out explaining that my symbols stood for joy in my new work and trepidation about failing. I don't really remember. What I do remember is her attack on my marriage.

She took the opportunity to berate me for being dominated by Harvey, referring to me as "little wifey." This was a term she often used for women who had given up on their own growth and aspirations. I was in shock. I struggled to cope with her dismissive view of my life and my marriage as my students and those I had encouraged to come to the workshop looked on. As group leader I could hardly undermine her authority. Yet I knew that what she was saying was biased. She hadn't spent time with Harvey and me for two years. How could she consider herself an authority on my life?

Maybe she was testing my humility as a disciple, insulting me the way she had attacked young Swami Sivananda in front of his students. Whatever her purpose, I didn't like it. Two years at the School of Social Work had taught me a new client-centred approach. It was important to engage the client in a process of respect. Empowerment was the basis of all interventions.

The workshop ended on Sunday afternoon. Instead of feeling reconnected with my guru and feeling the old sense of wholeness following time with her, I felt betrayed and misunderstood.

I said goodbye to the students with all the graciousness I could muster, wondering to myself what on earth they were thinking. The next morning I phoned Swami Radha at the house where she was staying. (In my two-year absence she had established her Toronto headquarters with a couple who were my neighbours and whom I had introduced to her teachings. She no longer stayed as a guest in my home.)

It was two days before she would talk with me on the phone. My script was carefully rehearsed. First I told her I was surprised that she thought she was an up-to-date expert on something as complex as my private life, since we had barely seen each other for two years. I went on to express my opinion that it was bad management on her part to degrade someone who was working on her behalf. It wasn't good for the group leader and it wasn't good for "business."

Having finished my part of the conversation I felt pleased with myself. I waited for her response, but none was coming.

She talked of other things—the people she had met during the past two days and the students who were coming for sessions with her that afternoon.

Months later I was shocked to hear her telling others that I was an exceptional person because I could accept criticism from my guru without getting upset or reacting to it angrily. She hadn't heard my pain and anger, let alone my message about being respectful to me.

In 1983, two years after that painful workshop, Shambhala House opened in the Beaches area of Toronto. This was to be an offshoot of the Yashodhara Ashram and was headed up by a former student of mine who had been made a swami by Swami Radha. There were two opening nights of celebration, and Swami Radha was in attendance.

Those who went the first night told me that she had started the evening by going around the circle, asking each person how they came to be there in Shambhala House. Each person talked about me. I had been their first yoga teacher. I had introduced them to her teachings through the dream group or through workshops.

I guess she wasn't pleased by my prominence in forming this community. The second evening, which I attended, started out differently. Swami Radha asked each person to give her name and no more. She was making sure I didn't become the obvious link between all these people and her new venture in Toronto. I was beginning to understand her need to prevent any competition. She saw me as a rival! How strange that felt, especially after all the years I had spent trying to cut my ego down to size and practise humility.

I made another attempt to connect with her. Maybe I could still profit from her teachings. Maybe I could work on my dreams with her. That sounded safe enough. In spite of my disappointment and anger with her I still missed her.

Here is an entry from my diary at the time.

Wednesday, Sept. 21, 1983
Went to see Swami Radha for a dream session. She had suggested a more in-depth study of dreams. I thought this sounded like a good idea, but I find I'm doing this for her, not for me. I had a weird dream about "suffer the little children to come unto me." It means nothing at all to me. It's a Swami Radha dream. [For me, it meant Swami Radha was influencing my dream life. For someone wanting to find her self, this was an unhealthy intrusion. Or maybe I was dreaming to please her—dreaming the sort of thing she'd be interested in.]

She was picking up accurately on my reactions to her competition. She told me I'm her equal and that I don't need her intrusion into my life (!???).

She offered to return my grandmother's pin that I had given to her. I do want it back and said so.

By this time I had started Focusing, the next step in my journey of healing. Now my guidance was coming both from Focusing and dreams. One expanded on the other. Before falling asleep I would ask for a dream. During the day I would pay attention to my body's physical response to a particular situation.

I had had a series of Focusing experiences involving birds. This was the way my unconscious spoke to me, providing direction for my next step in life.

Friday, Sept. 24, 1983
Focusing on all that about Swami Radha. A big, majestic bird is curled up in my abdomen. It grows to fill my neck and thorax with its body. Then I feel relief. A message comes. *You have to let it fly. Don't keep it inside.* There's a

sense of a hundred birds flying up and out of me. A feeling of lightness and freedom.

What's the crux of all this? *You lost your grandmother and now you're losing Swami Radha. You had got her back and now you're losing her again. You know Swami Radha won't let you leave in peace. She'll hang onto you.*

Let her hang on if she needs to. But I have to be clear in my head. It wasn't right to let her "muddle in my affairs," as she says in her German way.

That night: a dream about a bird. I'd asked for further clarification and had another dream with a bird symbol.

I open a window. There is a storm window, a second pane of glass. A large bird has been held between the two panes. It is dead and falls to the ground as I open the window. It seems to be a large seagull. I feel no remorse. It was dead before I got here, being held up by two panes.

Sunday, Sept. 26, 1983
I ask Harvey to help me with the bird symbols. "What do birds signify?" he asks me. "Freedom," I reply immediately. These are all trapped birds. Birds are free, soar above it all, they have a heightened perspective.

They depend on the earth for sustenance, though. They bridge the two worlds. They soar and then come back for food and water and to rest. They rear their young and perform their practical work here on earth.

My bird can't soar. It's being held, trapped in my body or between two panes of glass.

I was ready for a new stage in my life, one of freedom to connect to my own wisest self.

Chapter 9

Becoming a Therapist

Soon after graduation I entered my first 10k running race. During my years studying social work I'd taken up running to reduce my stress level. Starting with walking and running around my neighbourhood I'd worked up gradually to much longer runs. Yoga, with its development of flexibility, and running, with its development of cardiovascular strength, were the perfect combination for keeping me fit.

My first competitive run, the Brooks Spring Runoff, sponsored by Brooks Shoes, was through High Park. I turned up wearing the shorts, top, and head scarf I had used for painting the house. Imagine my surprise when I came second in the Women's Masters Division and found myself up on the podium with other runners sporting club ribbons and smart clothes. I won a new pair of shoes. Being a fast runner did wonders for my self-esteem at this critical time in my life. Running long distances regularly with Harvey relaxed my body and instilled in me a sense of my own strength.

In those early days some clients mystified me. I especially remember a young blonde woman who came to me with a sexual problem. She had moved in with her boyfriend of two years. Sex had been great as long as they lived apart. Now that they were in a committed relationship, whenever he approached her sexually, her body went numb. Often she was unaccountably frightened. Today, if I heard that story I would wonder about child sexual abuse.

Then there was the young woman who told me that she felt sexually aroused when we talked about her mother. I knew nothing about women sexually abusing children and so I was as perplexed as she. Today I would create a safe place for her to explore those erotic feelings about the woman who raised her.

What we don't know about, we often don't recognize. I still wonder about those clients whom I could not help. I just hope they eventually found a therapist who recognized their symptoms and helped them recover from child sexual abuse.

In those early days mainstream therapists weren't interested in child sexual abuse. Then, during the women's movement and when the Vietnam War veterans returned, awareness of psychological trauma exploded. Soldiers were returning with post-traumatic stress disorder and were unable to fit back into the American society they had fought for. Nobody wanted to listen to their horror stories. They refused to be silenced, forming their own "rap groups" and opening a Pandora's box of psychological trauma. At the same time the women's movement broke the silence about the child abuse that was endemic to our society. Women began sharing their secrets about the physical, emotional, and sexual abuse they had endured as helpless children in their own homes, schools, and churches.

In the early seventies Harvey was one of the first mainstream psychotherapists to believe in and learn about child sexual abuse. He was working as a child psychiatry resident at the Hincks Treatment Centre in Toronto, a child and adolescent treatment centre, when he met fourteen-year-old Shirley Turcotte. Shirley was a suicidal teenager who revealed to him the sexual horrors of her childhood. Fortunately both Harvey and his supervisor, Dr. Angus Hood, were open to believing the unthinkable. Before long Harvey was treating a handful of youngsters who had been sexually abused in their homes. Other staff members began to joke that he was either indulging in a bizarre interest or planting sexual suggestions in the minds of his young patients. After all, the current psychiatric text said that child sexual abuse was something the psychiatrist would not likely see in his practice, since it occurred in only one in a million families.

As is acknowledged today, child sexual abuse is so common that all of us know men and women in our own social circles who were abused as children. It is society's best-kept secret—something nobody knows about but to which everyone is exposed.

Shirley Turcotte went on to become one of Canada's leading experts in treating sexual abuse. When no treatment existed Shirley set up support groups in Vancouver for survivors and developed programs aimed at helping them deal with their pain, shame, and rage.

Nine years after Shirley had been my husband's patient she wrote to him from her home in Vancouver that she wanted to reconnect on a social basis. Harvey considered her request and wrote back that he would be open to a new non-professional relationship, providing I was included. Shirley came to stay the weekend with us. She and I were immediately drawn to each other.

Shirley wanted to learn Focusing. She saw how useful it would be both for herself and for the survivors she was helping.

We made a deal. I would teach Shirley Focusing and she would teach me about sexual abuse. Thus began a time of new learning for both of us. Shirley was travelling a lot, sharing her knowledge with others. When she was in Toronto, which was often, she stayed with us and we continued to trade skills and understanding.

I remember attending the Canadian Psychiatric Association meetings in Banff, Alberta, during this time. A brave young female psychiatry resident presented a paper on the possibility of encountering sexual abuse in one's practice. I recall how her supervisor stood close to her, attempting to lend credibility to the audacious paper. It was a very timid, cautious presentation. I was struck again with Shirley's knowledgeable grasp of the signs, symptoms, and treatment that actually helped survivors.

Once I was trained to recognize the prevalence of sexual abuse I realized a number of my clients were survivors. Learning from Shirley, from the sparse written material available, and from Harvey's experiences, I was amazed to discover I really understood their feelings of shame and rage. I was surprisingly good at this work. What's more I shared a number of the characteristics on the lists of signs and symptoms. Those aren't only about sexual abuse, I thought. I feel those things, too. I reasoned that religious repression could play a role.

One thing Shirley impressed on Harvey and me was how little support she had been given in her efforts to make a life for herself. No one, except Harvey in his professional role, had taken an interest in her. With no parents and no nurturing adults she had really been on her own. While she was Harvey's patient she supported herself by working two jobs and living alone in a basement apartment so she could attend high school at Jarvis Collegiate Institute. One day she was called to the principal's office. He explained to her that he had been told she had no parents and was living in an illegal basement apartment, so nobody was paying taxes for her to attend school. Therefore she could no longer attend school there. At the time Shirley felt like all avenues were now blocked to her. No matter how hard she worked she could never make it without help from some adults with clout.

In our talks years later Shirley made it clear to Harvey and me that good kids who have been abused and who struggle on their own need a little more than just caring professional care. We listened and began our own experience of trying to provide some adult protection for two deserving young people.

Our experience with taking abused teenagers into our home started one Christmas when Harvey was working at the Youthdale Crisis Service, a Toronto lock-up for violent and emotionally disturbed teens. Not all the youth fell into that category. Some simply needed a safe place to live. Fourteen-year-old Ellen was one of those kids. Child protective services removed her from her home when her father was charged with sexually abusing her. She had recently moved into a new group home. She wasn't allowed to go home for Christmas to her abusive family and, being new, didn't know anyone at the group home.

Harvey told me the heart-wrenching story of this bright, nice kid who was all alone at Christmas. Could we include her in our family Christmas? A rush of compassion warmed my heart. Of course she could be with us.

Harvey arrived home with Ellen before noon on December 25. My mother and I were preparing Christmas dinner. Frank, who was twelve at the time, took Ellen under his wing. He was enjoying having another kid in the house at Christmastime.

I extricated myself from the dinner preparations long enough to greet her. She looked up at me from under her dark hair, her brown eyes half expecting rejection. I recognized her as a

First Nations child. Dressed in a light blue and white chequered jumper that Children's Aid had provided, she took off, relieved, with Frank as he led the way to his new Pac-Man game.

During dinner she had tears in her eyes much of the time. I guess she was thinking of her own family, the family that had adopted her from her birth mother. When she was a baby Children's Aid had taken Ellen from her mother. Her new mother had left her and her siblings alone and untended while she went drinking. Now the Children's Aid had intervened once more, fourteen years later, following Ellen's attempted suicide in her adoptive home. Her adoptive father and other men of the family allegedly had exploited her for sexual purposes.

At the end of Christmas Day I said goodbye to Ellen, little realizing she was destined to become a major figure in my life over the following years.

She started turning up in the middle of the night, cold and scared. Harvey would get out of bed and settle her in our guest room for the night. I, too, agreed there was nothing else to do. We couldn't turn her out on the streets. During this time she was attached to one worker after the other, but a worker is not a mother. Ellen needed more. She began staying with us for longer periods of time. Each of us, Harvey, Frank, and I, grew to care deeply for this courageous, damaged young person. Finally Harvey and I started thinking seriously of legally adopting her. She dreamed of becoming a physician and had the brains to achieve her vision. My heart went out to her, seeing her studying for her correspondence courses and getting one hundred percent in mathematics. I felt compelled to give her the opportunity to make something of her life.

With our commitment and her increasing safety came the terrible eruption of her past. It was as if she was determined to smash anything good in her life. I can only guess at the terrible pain she could now feel towards both her adoptive and her birth mother. She started drinking paint thinner, weed-control poison, anything she could find in our house with which to harm herself. Time after time we rushed her to the emergency room to have her stomach pumped. She overdosed. She shot up with street drugs. She was drawn to predatory men.

I still shudder with the memory of taking her to Sunnybrook Hospital after an overdose. The young male psychiatrist came in to talk to her. She wouldn't talk. I felt I had to do the talking for her. I began with what, to me, was a very complex tale.

"Ellen has had a lifetime of bad experiences," I said.

The psychiatrist looked decidedly impatient. "Just tell me what happened today," he said. 'Why is she here?"

Clearly he viewed her as chronic: someone who would be in and out of hospital all her life. No use spending a lot of time on this one. Just pump her stomach and discharge her until the next time.

"Please," I wanted to plead. "This is Ellen. She's a really good person. She needs patience and help."

I could see it was no use. I also felt embarrassed to be viewed as a foolish woman who was championing a lost cause.

Over the years Ellen's lack of judgment got her raped and drugged, repeatedly. I remember Harvey getting up in the middle of the night to let her in after one of her unsavoury dates had dropped her off at our house. I heard her go into our washroom by the front door and I wanted to scream, "No, don't let her use our bathroom." But I just went back to bed and pretended to sleep, paralyzed by the tension between my own need for a safe home and my need to rescue Ellen.

Ellen hadn't yet reached the height of acting out her rage against the past when Linda showed up. Linda was another good kid who had had a terrible life. She was living in a lean-to she'd built for herself in a ravine. But winter was coming. Her mother had many children, all by different men. Linda handled her rage and confusion over her mother by "killing her." She told all of us her mother had died. It was many months before my husband realized there had been no funeral for a dead mother. Sometimes both girls were with us at the same time.

Linda was as guarded and anti-social as Ellen was charming and fun. Linda tended to hide in her bedroom, our guest-room. She was a homely girl, ill at ease in her heavy body and not interested in makeup or attractive clothing. She suffered from dissociative identity disorder, which meant she had what's called an alter—a split-off part of the personality that functions independently of the affected individual. Linda's alter existed for sex. This other part of her was outrageously sexual with Harvey. I would enter his study to see her looking seductively at him, trying to persuade him to succumb to her charms. He, for his part, would just continue at his desk, doing what he was doing in an attempt to assure the alter there was no chance of anything happening.

Linda also had terrible nightmares. One night Frank wakened me. He was up late studying for exams and heard groans and screams from Linda, who was asleep.

"Mom," he said. "Wake up. Linda's having terrible nightmares."

It didn't occur to him to wake his father, who was Linda's doctor. Mom was the parent who soothed you in the night if you were sick or had a nightmare. This is where professional life intersected with personal family life. Was Linda a patient or a child of the family? But this was not the time to debate such issues of professional boundaries versus family life.

I went into Linda's room to waken her. I touched her. She bolted upright, screamed, jumped out of bed with the strength of a terrified wild animal, and headed in her nightgown for our front door. It was a cold winter night, yet somehow she managed to unlock the door and flee barefoot in the snow out into the dark night.

By now Harvey had appeared in his dressing gown. He chased after her in the darkness of the night.

When Harvey and Linda were safely home I returned to bed, sad for Linda's tragic terrors, furious for the disruption to my home, upset that my son's studying was disturbed, and angry with my husband for bringing this tension and distress into our home. I hoped, too, that none of the neighbours had witnessed my husband in his dressing gown chasing a young girl in a flannel nightgown down our street.

Linda, like Ellen, resided with us off and on for years. Harvey spent most of his free time dealing with the girls' myriad problems. Our home sometimes felt like the annex of the Youthdale Crisis Service. I felt I had lost my husband. He was too busy dealing with their fascinating multiple personalities. He was no longer interested in the ordinary annoyances or frustrations I might have.

I was bursting with outrage. I would yell at him and threaten to leave the house myself if they didn't leave. Then I would feel bad about my behaviour. After all I was so fortunate and had so much. I needed to be more loving and generous. This would be followed with an apology to him and reassurance that I supported the overriding importance of keeping these two youngsters alive.

And so I would stuff my hurt, resentment, and rage down deep in my belly, determined to be a good and loving woman. I wanted to do good in the world. I wanted to be generous and loving. I castigated myself for not being big enough to give these worthwhile girls a place in my home and my heart.

But there was another force at work I didn't know about. A deeper, more terrible force was wrapping its tentacles around my life energy, choking me into silence and, alternately, causing eruptions of burst blood and guts to spatter on the walls of my life.

During the time we were dealing with Ellen and Linda I knew nothing of my own sexual abuse. Maybe their presence in my house would have been bad enough even if I'd had an ideal upbringing. Or, more likely, if I'd had a healthy start in life it would have been clear to me from the start that two disturbed patients of my husband did not belong in my home. As it was, their pain and distress stirred the dirty stew of memories I held in my own belly. They brought the helplessness of victims with them. My house was filled with muffled screams and the terror of victimization. The vibrations of their fear resonated in my own body. I was constantly agitated, my sleep was disturbed, and I moved as if I were wading waist deep in a warm polluted pool. I could no longer find myself. I was lost, struggling to move through a sludge of conflicted emotions.

Child sexual abuse! It drove me crazy to think of all the children who were enslaved and trapped in the soft seduction of predatory persuasion. I understood how children were groomed by a skilled pedophile, who would begin with befriending the victim until he or she viewed the abuser first as a best friend and finally as a love object. I even understood the child's fierce loyalty to a predator. Only children who lacked a trusting relationship with a non-exploitative adult could succumb to a predator. I knew all of this. Yet I did not know how I myself had been betrayed in childhood by a father and grandfather who exploited my vulnerability and by a mother who valued her perception of her perfect family over my safety.

The agony and desperation of Ellen and Linda reached into the layers of pain packed away in my belly, stirring it around and making it rise to the surface. I started to feel the anguish of something that had happened to me a long time ago. My layers of perception were opened to new stirrings.

It was a couple of years later that Harvey and I, with no Ellen or Linda in our lives, decided to stay home at Christmas and Focus. This is when my own memories of child sexual abuse made themselves known. Thus it is for thousands of other survivors. When life is good, when our mates are there for us at last, the horrid memories of the past are free to surface. It is as if the memories say, "Ah, you are ready for us now."

When I set up my fledgling practice as a clinical social worker I sought out a supervisor, an expert to whom the less-experienced practitioner brings cases and discusses difficulties in dealing with clients. One of my early supervisors was Henry Regehr. Like me, he was trained as a social worker. Unlike me, he had twenty years' experience in dealing with individuals, couples, and families. He was one of the early Canadian social workers to establish a successful private practice, the sort of practice I wanted to have. Sessions with him provided the backbone for my unsure beginnings as a therapist.

Supervision sessions with Henry frequently stirred strangely uncomfortable feelings in my gut. Henry would ask, "How would your family have handled that?" Or "If that had happened in your family, how would the different members have reacted?"

My head knew these were good questions, meant to help me understand what was happening in term of my clients. But whenever Henry asked about my family I experienced a sinking feeling in my belly, followed by a ringing in my head. My brain filled with white clouds. I was unable to feel, think, or articulate thoughts. I felt like a dolt. In those days I did not know about dissociation. I was just embarrassed and bewildered that I appeared so stupid.

Looking back at my journal entries of that time I remember struggling with the married couples I was counselling in those early days.

June 25, 1982

Letting Henry in: If he's going to help me, I have to let him in on very personal feelings and memories. I'm having difficulty with the new couple. I'm not handling the case well. I realize I'm getting into my own stuff.

Henry asks a lot of questions that are hard to answer, but today in our session I got a whole new awareness of why I'm a marriage counsellor.

My sense of being to blame for my father's sadness: It's my fault.

Memory of protecting him from my mother's anger: My spontaneous rush of feeling that she mustn't hurt him.

My role in the family was to charm him and keep him with us.

Motivation for marital counselling: I want them to settle amicably. This distorted my view with the new couple. I don't want them to be angry and destructive. I have to keep them happy.

Identification with my father: When I was small, my mother always said, "She's just like her father." Am I? I consider this an attempt to push us together.

I'm having a hard time staying neutral and not trying to rescue the men in the couple situation.

More journal notes on that painful session with Henry:

Henry said: "Your father lost the love of his life in England."
I felt enormous sadness.

Compare this with my pleasure when the men I'm work-ing with set themselves free to be with the woman they love.

My guilt: I caused my father to stay. He finally died, strangled by staying. I just couldn't do enough to keep him happy. I had to amuse him, be his companion.

Henry on the way I keep him out in supervision: "If you let me in, then I'd get to know Mary and wouldn't that be a shame."

My realization that it's a taboo to think and feel about my father: I'm also defending against the pain of talking about him. To have felt my restlessness would have smashed the system that held us all together in our family roles.

Henry on my mother: She had to convince him (my father) he'd made the right choice (by always dressing well and catering to him).

Henry wonders if I answer his questions the way my father would have. Little spurts of well-controlled infor-mation and then silence. (At the time I disagreed—but I expect I do react like my father.) Plus the fact that at that moment my thoughts close down and my feelings are no longer accessible.

Henry wants to know about transference. Do I experi-ence Henry as my father? At the time I said I didn't—that my transference was more Harvey to Henry. But in recon-sidering—Henry's upper body is my father's. His chest at my eye level.

How strange it is for me to look back at these writings. It's as if my psyche was preparing me little by little for the key to my fears and anxieties.

My journal entry written two days later reads:

Sunday, June 27, 1982
Yesterday—heavy, depressed mood—big lump in my abdomen and throat. Couldn't shake it. Finally told Harvey at night. He'd known something was wrong and also that I wasn't mad at him. Our closeness (sex), long sleep, and here I am feeling a lot better.

The first crack in my image of an idealized father came five years later when my father had been dead for sixteen years.

There was a conference on adolescent psychiatry being held in San Juan, Puerto Rico. We decided to attend as a family. My husband, now an adolescent psychiatrist, had spent some of his teen years living and going to school in Puerto Rico. I had never been to the Caribbean.

Frank and I would go off sightseeing while Harvey attended meetings. One day, though, a paper was being given on the Moonies and other spiritual cults that were attracting young people. This was of particular interest to Frank, who had won a public speaking contest with his research on the subject.

We turned up for the paper and were told the program had been altered. First we would have to sit through a paper on treating the children of alcoholics. We settled in to wait for the really interesting presentation on cults.

That first paper shook my world. Children of alcoholics, I was told, are hard to obtain treatment for because they are very good kids. They don't cause trouble and therefore do not stand out. Some of the characteristics are the following: The children go to bizarre lengths to prevent the alcoholic from becoming angry, believing that the anger causes the drinking. If Dad gets angry about his morning newspaper being wet, the child will get up early enough to make sure the paper stays dry. In a treatment centre they are the peacemakers who, if there is one towel short, will surrender their own rather than let anyone get upset.

When I got home from the conference I turned to the recent literature on adult children of alcoholics. It was the first time any literature had been relevant to my own difficulties in life. Help for adult children of alcoholics was available years before anything was written for survivors of other kinds of abuse. The descriptions of dysfunctional families portrayed in the literature were meant for those who had grown up in alcoholic homes, but they're common to any kind of abuse. I certainly recognized my own family's adherence to the three rules: *don't feel, don't think, don't talk.* What I had always considered the behaviour of a "nice" family turned out to be pathological. For the trauma survivor, the dysfunctional feels normal.

It was a lot to take in.

Chapter 10

Rethinking Yoga

During the decade I studied with Swami Radha I experienced the comfort of attachment to a loving, encouraging figure. I grew in this relationship. I gained from my close connection with my guru. But there was a price to pay.

Growth for the disciple means becoming more like the guru, who, in turn, strives to be more like her own guru. I believed that o be loved I believed I had to behave in ways that fit the East's system of gurus and disciples. The East does not value individuality. It was a long time before I realized that I was repeating the same dynamic I had been struggling to escape from with my mother. I had to de-self my authentic self and become the person the guru valued, just as I had tried to lop off any parts of me that didn't fit with my mother's wish for a perfect daughter. In the end, as I matured and became more true to myself, I had to break off the close relationship with Swami Radha.

Fortunately, unlike many other disciples who leave emotionally whipped by an angry guru and take years to lick their wounds and recover, she and I parted company on more amiable grounds. Maybe this was because she had always reassured me that no matter what path I took in the future, she would give me her blessings. Perhaps she decided to save face and behave as if nothing had happened between us. At any rate she later invited me to come for a holiday at the ashram.

The visit took place a year after that fateful workshop. In a generous gesture of reconciliation she invited me to come as her guest and not as a disciple. I stayed in the log guest house on the hill, the scene of fond memories during the three-month teachers' course. She made it clear she did not expect me to attend evening *satsang* (devotional service) or behave as a humble disciple. I could be there on my own terms.

On this return journey I re-encountered Terence, whom I had known for years throughout many stages of his life as a disciple of Swami Radha. He was a handsome, dark-haired Englishman who brought to Canada his passion for First Nations people, teepees, and shamanism. He found a place on the shores of Kootenay Lake in Swami Radha's ashram. There he erected a teepee and swore his dedication to his shaman, Swami Radha.

When I first met him he was a humble devotee. But on this visit Terence had been exiled to an isolated cabin on the property. His meals were delivered to him in silence. He was allowed no communication with fellow devotees. He had shaved his head as a sign of repentance and humiliation. I'm not sure why he chose this way to show his repentance. I expect it was meant as a sign to Swami Radha that good-looking Terence valued her forgiveness more than his appearance. I also never found out the reason he was exiled. Probably it was for a forbidden romance with a woman visitor to the ashram.

When I arrived at the ashram to find Terence in solitary confinement I felt deeply sorry for him. I could understand his penitent's attitude, because I understood the culture of the ashram. He must be suffering terribly, I told myself.

Next came a written request from Terence delivered by a messenger, asking me to come and talk to him. Within moments a second message was delivered to my room in the guest house by another messenger. This message came from Swami Radha. If I spoke with Terence, it said, I must report everything we talked about to her. By now I was clear on my own commitment to client-centred work in counselling and the sacredness of confidentiality.

I immediately let Terence know the terms Swami Radha had decreed. After all, *he* was trying to win her forgiveness and acceptance again. As for me there was no way I was going to be the guru's spy. Not unexpectedly, Terence sent a message back that he would forgo a meeting with me.

Months later Terence turned up in Toronto. He was gaunt with weight loss, his skinniness made all the more evident by his shaved head. He carried his tail between his legs. He had run away from Swami Radha.

A good friend took him in and gave him a place to start his recovery. The healing began. Terence worked hard at extricating himself from his need for an external authority. He sought professional help and enrolled in a course to find employment.

The guy who shaved his head and swore obedience to a guru ended up being successful in the investment world. He bought land near the ashram, developed a community of caring friends, and won the respect of many.

Rita, to my mind, is a sadder story. She was an Ottawa mother of two teenagers and the wife of Tom, a civil servant. Swami Radha explained to Rita that she was a slave in her marriage.

As a stay-at-home mother, her life was filled with menial tasks. Rita believed she was destined for loftier purposes.

Convinced she was meant to serve a higher cause Rita left Tom and their children and moved into Many Mansions, Swami Radha's beautiful B.C. home. Now Rita was near her guru, right at the heart of spiritual growth.

Tom was encouraged to visit. I remember him as a weak, defeated sort of man. Maybe that was projection on my part, but that's how I perceived the situation.

Sadly, Tom died of a heart attack soon after. Following his death Swami Radha initiated Rita into swamihood. Rita became Swami Padmananda. Her spiritual growth was celebrated in the ceremony that bestowed this honour.

As the years passed it became obvious that the new swami had an alcohol problem. Her self-effacing little giggle was more about the sherry she had consumed than about the wit of her guru.

My observation was that Rita, Swami Padmananda, was an unfortunate woman who had rebelled against her role as a dependent woman with a husband and two children, only to become Swami Radha's "little wifey." Rita/Swami Padmananda washed the guru's undergarments and blouses. She intercepted phone calls, opened the mail, and brought the swami her tea. She dutifully followed Swami Radha everywhere, discreetly disappearing when the swami wanted privacy.

There were many others who experienced attachment to the mother figure of Swami Radha but didn't manage to move to the next stages of Western human development: individuation and separation. These stages were not recognized as desirable or healthy by those at the ashram.

Many years have passed since those heady days of studying with Swami Radha. Enlightenment was always just around the corner. Try a little harder. Don't slack off. You're almost there. It was exciting. It took a long time for me to realize that the teachings of my guru's scriptures were meant for celibate monks. They were about an ideal, not really attainable by those of us who want to live with mates and children, go to work, and live and love in the world outside the shelter of an ashram.

One aspect of my guru's teachings I am now critical of is her stance on sex. The "lower body" was to be suppressed. The urges of the sex drive were "animal" and to be sublimated into good works and giving to others. This may work for swamis and Roman Catholic priests, but in my opinion it is not adaptive in our society. Swami Radha didn't do my marriage any good. She made no secret that she considered those burdened by a spouse and children to be disadvantaged in the search for spiritual enlightenment. My numb body and my lack of interest in sex were viewed as a sign of a more evolved consciousness, not as a sign of a serious problem.

It wasn't until I began studying for my master's of social work that I understood sexuality was an enjoyable and normal act for a healthy young woman. How liberating that was. I had permission to set free my sexual passion! Those who had studied sexuality and who were authorities on mental and physical health said so. Thank goodness I finally was able to convince myself to let go and enjoy this god-given "glue" for long-term marriages.

I worry that New Age types and people who embrace the thinking of the East are failing to perceive some of the ways in which Eastern philosophy and psychology are not right for our culture. We hunger for the East's peace and tranquility, its lack of greed and materialism. Yet there are dangers. Surrendering the ego may sound like the path to serenity. But you need a strong and solid ego, in the Western sense, before surrendering it. You may end up with no self and just a hyper-critical super ego—like so many sincere spiritual aspirants.

There needs to be an understanding, too, of the word "ego." In the East it refers to the small, mean self. We are encouraged to be more aware, more present, more mature. All of this is good. But it is too often confused with the Western "ego," which is the person's true self, the authentic person.

To be successful in our Western culture a person needs a strong ego, in the way Western psychology defines it. We encourage our youth to leave home and create their own place in the world. We call it individuating and separating. It is necessary to become separate from your parents in order to mate with another and make this adult relationship central to your life. Economically and mentally we expect our young people to become self-sufficient and independent from the older generation.

In the West we value individuality. We praise the thinker who comes up with original thoughts and the artist who develops new art forms. This is very different from the Eastern spiritual teachings where a painter, for instance, tries to paint a lotus as much like the great classical artists as possible. Innovation is a deviation from perfection. It is not desirable. A seeker attempts to be as much like the guru as possible. The guru meanwhile is trying to be like his or her guru, who is trying to be more like God.

There are many traps in embracing Eastern asceticism. We need to be clear about which parts of the teachings are right for those of us living in our society. We need to be aware of our society's need for individuality. We need to take only what is right for us, with an awareness of what is not life-enhancing for a Westerner.

We also need to recognize what may not be indications of heightened spirituality but signs of a mental disorder resulting from childhood trauma. When I was studying yoga with Swami Radha I actually envied those fellow aspirants who spaced out in meditation and had to be brought back to the present by their friends. I listened with admiration to the woman who described how she knew she had been up in the night cooking but had no memory of her nocturnal activities. I wished fervently for something remarkable to happen to me. It was an absolute peak experience for me when, one day in yoga class, I found myself floating on the ceiling looking down at myself and the other students. I kept hoping for this to happen again.

It never did and I was disappointed. Today I would be very careful to discourage anyone's tendencies towards "floatiness."

When I was a small, helpless child, floating helped me escape from what was intolerable and inescapable. As an adult I am not powerless and my life events are certainly not intolerable. I don't want to be out of my body, numb and unfeeling. I want to feel and be present to the people and events in my life.

Today I view such "spiritual" happenings as signs of wounding—the traumatized person's way of escaping into dissociation. Many come to yoga for the same reasons I was attracted to it. They are looking for a way to calm their overactive nervous systems and gain some control over the irrational fear coursing through their bellies.

Swami Radha used to say that all mystics had been abused as children. Through hyper-vigilance and coping with their terrifying environments as children, mystics were merely people who had sharpened their five senses beyond what was considered normal. Swami Radha used the analogy of adults, children, and the cookie jar. Children cannot figure out how the adults know they have been into the cookie jar. This is because children do not perceive that the lid is on crooked and there are cookie crumbs on the kitchen counter. Mystics are like the adults and the rest of us are the children who wonder how on earth they know what they know.

I did not understand then that the coping skills that made me highly perceptive about what others were thinking and feeling originated in child sexual abuse.

Chapter 11

Focusing

I had figured out how to keep yoga in my life without jeopardizing my personal growth and autonomy. Still, the question remained: How could I bring to my counselling work the richness I experienced in yoga?

The pieces of the puzzle started coming together one day in the winter of 1981 when I was preparing lunch in my kitchen and listening to an interview on the radio. A psychologist was talking about an approach he'd developed called Focusing. "Focusing happens in the body," he was saying. "It's not enough to understand something with your head. We have to bring about change in the physical body. Without that, people don't really change."

I couldn't believe my ears. This sounded like what I'd been looking for! He said his model was psychologically sound in Western terms.

"We live life in our bodies," he went on. "Every situation we're in, everything we think or feel, the body is always responding. Usually in our society we ignore those bodily felt signals. Yet they're the pathway to our deeper knowing, to a level of consciousness not usually available to us."

My mother was visiting us that day and just then she entered the kitchen. To have ignored her and continued listening to the radio would have been viewed as an act of rudeness. I turned the radio off but scribbled the words "Focusing" and "Eugene Gendlin" before turning to pay attention to her.

Gendlin had mentioned a paperback published by Bantam called *Focusing*. I started a search for the book and finally located it months later. I was excited by what I read. This was exactly what I needed and what my clients needed. I liked the gentle attitude towards one's self. Focusing offered a way of being with problems without being overwhelmed by them. It relied on the body's physically felt responses to determine what was right for each unique organism in the universe. It taught that we have the answers inside us. We don't need an outside authority to tell us how to live our lives.

All these years I'd been working hard at changing myself into someone more acceptable, and now this Gendlin guy was telling me I was fine just as I was and would become more fine the closer I came to my authentic being. My authentic being! Not the perfect daughter, the perfect wife, or the ideal disciple. Just who I actually was—whoever that may be.

For several months I worked from the paperback, teaching myself to Focus. The results were gratifying, but I couldn't be sure I was doing it right until I found someone who was familiar with this approach.

When I heard a Focusing weekend was to be held at a retreat centre near Toronto I signed up immediately. The weekend was led by two Roman Catholic priests, Peter Campbell and Ed McMahon. Here was my opportunity to investigate first-hand whether Focusing was really as amazing as I hoped.

As soon as I arrived at the Queen of Apostles Renewal Centre, a huge, old, red brick building sprawled over a picturesque property that sloped to the river below, I was assigned a tiny, spartan bedroom.

About fifty of us gathered in a large room to begin the weekend. Most were Roman Catholic nuns, priests, and parishioners. These participants felt secure being there because two priests were in charge. As for me I wondered if I were in the right place. Would I really learn about Focusing? Or would this be too religious for my purposes?

When Pete and Ed, as the two priests are affectionately known, introduced themselves, they described how they came to embrace Focusing. Both had been psychologists before entering the priesthood in Ottawa. Naturally they were both assigned the role of therapist to troubled nuns and priests. What the two psychologist priests found was that the sicker their patients became, the more they prayed and the more they attended mass. The fact that their patients weren't getting better struck them as very strange, since they assumed that mass was good and prayer was healing.

Exploring the issue they decided these good Catholics were praying "from the neck up." They were saying the words and going through the actions but nothing was happening inside them. They were totally cut off from their bodies and therefore from their own spiritual connection.

Somehow they needed to connect with their physical selves. After all we know we are feeling a given emotion because we feel it in our bodies. It was this search that led Pete and Ed to Eugene Gendlin's work. Here was a way you could actually teach people to realize they were alive inside their bodies, that there was something worth paying attention to in the body.

After the two priests had introduced Focusing to the whole group we were divided into small groups to actually try some Focusing. Following the group leader to whom I was assigned I went off with five others into a separate room. Our leader was a matronly blonde who seemed very tentative. Each of us would be led through the six steps of Focusing, she explained.

She began to lead the first participant. Oh no, I thought, our leader was reading the instructions off a paper. This did not bode well. I sat there, hoping I would still be able to experience this method I was putting so much hope in.

When it was my turn she began leading me through the first step of Focusing. It is called "Clearing Space," in which you ask yourself what comes between you and feeling really wonderful. When something comes up you just acknowledge it without getting caught up in it and then put it outside your body.

I did as she instructed for a few minutes. But then a red balloon appeared in my mind's eye. I was mentally holding it by a string. The instructor told me to put it down.

No way! I wasn't putting this down.

At that point I cut her out and concentrated on my red balloon, ignoring her voice telling me to put it on the floor. The essence of the red balloon was filling my whole torso. My lower body seemed to be reorganizing itself. It was as if a log cabin were being built inside my belly. My abdomen was solid and grounded. My upper body expanded with a benign peace and a sense of wisdom greater than my own. I felt connected to something very powerful. I giggled to myself about this being an entirely unexpected spiritual experience. I felt huge, like the Michelin Man. My body was telling me in no uncertain terms that Focusing was right for me.

By the end of the retreat I knew I had to meet this Eugene Gendlin, the psychologist who wrote the book and whom I had heard interviewed on the radio. I needed to learn from him. His approach was intriguingly simple and yet so profound.

I wrote to the address given on the paperback: the Department of Behavioral Sciences at the University of Chicago. In time I received a large envelope of photocopied articles and items of interest. One announced a weekend training session coming up with Gendlin. I had to go. I registered and prepared to sit at the feet of my new guru.

At the appointed time I flew to Chicago. I turned up at the university's Center for International Studies wearing my best professional suit, my patent-leather pumps, and carrying my black leather briefcase. I was expecting to take my place in an auditorium among a couple of hundred others who would be drawn here by Gendlin's brilliance.

Instead I was shown to a small sitting room where a dozen chairs waited in a circle. Nervousness spread over my body. I was going to sit here, close to my psychological hero. In an attempt to control my anxiety I concentrated on every detail. There was a man in a tartan shirt and jeans smoking a cigarette at the door. Probably a janitor, I thought. I noticed his socks didn't match. People were beginning to arrive, all of them dressed very casually. I was starting to feel self-conscious about my professional attire and more and more intimidated by the prospect of being in such an intimate setting with Dr. Gendlin.

The janitor finished his cigarette and entered the room. He sat down in our circle. I realized, judging from the interest and respect shown to him by the other participants, he had to be Eugene Gendlin.

We introduced ourselves and Gendlin started in with what he thought Focusing was all about.

"You see," he said, crossing his legs, leaning forward intently to look around the circle to make sure we understood, "you are separate from your problems and your issues. You are also separate from your emotions. You need to find the right distance from your problems so you can have a relationship with them. You can't do that if you're too close to your problems or too distant.

"Most people do one or the other. Either they can't find any space for themselves free of their problems, or they put so much distance between themselves and what bothers them, there's no way they can be effective in resolving their issues. We need to find the right distance. We do that by Clearing Space, the first step in Focusing."

The thought of feeling really good was revolutionary to me. I had always felt it wasn't okay to feel good. I needed to feel serious and reliable. A good person carries a burden of responsibility, I had told myself. I explored my discomfort a little more and discovered a belief that if I felt wonderful, something bad was bound to happen.

On the other hand there was a sense of relief that my problems were finite. I could always come to the end of the list and experience that, except for a few problems, everything was fine. The hovering sense of a heavy burden, weighing me down twenty-four hours a day, lifted. I could set down my burden and take a break from it.

That whole weekend was filled with life-changing challenges. Inside me there was an person who was different from the part of me that handled the external world, making my way through traffic or balancing my cheque book. While the outer self was the tip of the iceberg, the inner self was nine-tenths underwater. To access that deeper self I needed to be with it in a very caring, patient way. Otherwise it would not dare to tell me what I needed to know and I would continue to have access to only a fraction

of my wisdom. *It* knew what needed my attention. *It* knew how
to move towards healing. *I* didn't. This meant allowing the body
to lead the way while keeping my head out of it. All of this was
summed up in Gendlin's definition of the Focusing Attitude:
*Every bad feeling has in it the potential for a more right way
of being if we give it space to move towards its rightness.*

I needed to value the uncomfortable feelings. Instead of trying to get rid of them I was to view them with curiosity. The
queasy feeling in my stomach or the tight feeling in my chest
was trying to tell me something. If I could learn to Focus on
those bodily, felt signals I could tap into my unconscious knowing. I would know how I really felt about something or why
some seemingly trivial incident upset me.

Back home, after the weekend, I started teaching Focusing
to a few students.

My teacher-student relationship with Dr. Gendlin became
increasingly central to my life. He was planning to open the
Focusing Institute in Chicago. A year after the session in Chicago
he asked me if I would be interested in starting something in
Toronto. About that time Harvey decided to leave institutional
psychiatry and go into private practice. Together we opened
a suite of offices, the perfect setting for his group therapy for
parents with out-of-control adolescents and for my Focusing
centre. I began giving classes, training people, and running
weekend retreats.

Often while I was having a wonderful experience through
Focusing I was also paralyzed with my old, irrational fears.
I decided I was suffering from social phobia, a fear of being
exposed to others' negative opinions. It took courage for me to
go to just about any social event. If I didn't know the people
well, if I wasn't assured of their approval, I dreaded entering the
strange situation. Professional meetings and teaching, both of

which were becoming parts of my daily life, took their toll on my energy. My head understood that this anxiety was always in anticipation of an event. Once I got there and looked at the kind faces and ordinary humans I was joining, my fears subsided.

Since I had no idea why I was so fearful I decided to make this my Focusing project. In Focusing, the unconscious talks to one through images and words that arise spontaneously from the body's felt sense.

I sat quietly, asking my body how it felt when I was out in public and exposed to scrutiny. After a few minutes an ugly sense of rot and heaviness settled in my middle. "Ugly rot" were the words that matched the felt sense. These words are what Focusing calls a handle. Once you have a handle, you are well on the way to getting the message inherent in the felt sense. As I concentrated on the physical sensation an image arose that caught the essence of the ugly rot. It was Gollum, the scary creature from J.R.R. Tolkien's underworld.

I needed to get some distance from this malevolent-looking being. Finally I was able to isolate Gollum in a Plexiglas aquarium. Reassured that he was safely put away I went back inside to scrub where he'd been. With a figurative brush and plenty of soap and water I attempted to scour my middle. A circle of roots wanted to shoot up and fill the space and produce another Gollum. I poured in a caustic substance that checked their growth but didn't harm my body.

Meanwhile, the caged Gollum was looking very sad. As I watched him from my safe distance he became my father. He looked down with a mournful posture and a sorrowful look on his face. I felt an overwhelming urge to make everything okay for him by letting him come back inside me, but instead told him he had to stay inside the aquarium. He did not belong inside me. It wasn't right to kill Gollum but I also knew it was too dangerous to let him out of his enclosure. The best I could do was keep him caged.

I took Gollum to my next appointment with Helen, my psychotherapist. I explained to her how he had emerged out of my Focusing on my social phobia and how he was the unspeakably ugly, repulsive part of me. I told her he was dangerous and very clever. He wanted to destroy me. No matter how hard I tried Gollum wouldn't let me have a good life and feel good about myself. He constantly told me I wasn't supposed to have a good life.

"What would he do if you let him loose?" Helen asked.

I had a flash of him entering her or getting back inside me.

From somewhere inside me came a warning: "He's a malevolent being."

The warning voice was harsh—an internalized mother, not a soft inner voice.

From inside his aquarium Gollum looked sad. "I haven't done anything wrong," he whimpered.

Helen encouraged me to make friends with this unacknowledged part of myself. In the safety of her office I imagined I was Gollum. I became all soft and relaxed through my throat, jaw, and neck. I was enjoying playing this funny, wrinkled creature.

"Suppose you made a stocking puppet of him, what would he look like?"

"He'd have wrinkles and folds and ... uh ... pubic hair. Bulging eyes, too," I replied.

Once, during the days that followed, I imagined sitting in a darkened theatre with my mother. She looked over and saw, to her horror, Gollum sitting erect on my lap. I had a good laugh at her shock.

Over the next days the rotting feeling in my abdomen shifted. A shift occurs when the felt sense releases and, simultaneously, new knowing comes into one's awareness. I started having fun with Gollum instead of being afraid of him. I covered my hand and arm with a black sock and sewed eyes on my puppet. Gollum took on a life of his own, snuggling and wriggling happily on my lap and against my neck.

It felt like an incredibly joyous reunion with a part of myself I'd cut off. He was the answer to my dulled sexuality and to my social phobia. I was so hopeful. Without these problems life would be so beautiful.

Life, however, wasn't beautiful in the days that followed. My journals tell of even more anxiety. I dreamed of a forest with trees wrapped in huge snakes. Snakes don't belong on trees, I thought. The woods felt like a place of innocence, yet there were these dangerous snakes lying in wait, coiled on the trees.

I was still a long way from realizing the underlying cause of my fears and tensions. But like the proverbial drip on a rock, Focusing was bringing me closer and closer to my buried memories of child sexual abuse.

Meanwhile, in Chicago, Eugene Gendlin and those he had trained to teach Focusing were planning the first week-long retreat. (This was before the founding of the Focusing Institute and my Centre for Focusing in Toronto.) Mary McGuire, Dr. Gendlin's right-hand person, led the retreat. Dr. Gendlin came most afternoons to teach and work individually with participants.

This retreat, and the ones that followed, took place in a down-at-the-heels Roman Catholic retreat centre, The Villa Redeemer, set in a game preserve in suburban Chicago where deer came to the windows and roamed the woods.

There were six of us—all women. As women do, we became a very close-knit group with the exception of one who kept to herself.

For most of her life this woman had been an elementary-school teacher. She was raw with rage, stung with the injustice of having been fired from her job. Twenty-five years of her life she'd given to teaching children. But finally she hit a student hard across the face. And that ended her career. She thought it was so unfair. She'd endured the frustrations of working with those spoiled brats all those years.

The rest of us nurtured and supported each other, fully appreciative of Mary McGuire's wise and caring leadership. The aging teacher, though, gave Mary a hard time. Mary's way of teaching listening was all wrong. *She* had been trained in listening skills decades ago and knew the right way. She was angry with Mary and didn't hesitate to voice her criticisms.

The day it was her turn to work with Gene we all held our breath. What would happen?

She began telling the story all of us had heard so often about the insolent male student and her resorting to physical violence. Then she launched into a long complaint about Mary's leadership. Mary didn't know how to listen. *She* knew how to listen. She'd been listening for thirty years and now Mary was telling her she wasn't doing it right.

Gene received her with great understanding and gentleness. Yes of course she'd been listening for decades and knew a very good way of taking in what others had to say. And now *they* were coming along, telling her she didn't do it right. What did *they* know? He echoed her frustration and hurt.

I cast a glance over at Mary to see how she was taking this. She must have felt her boss wasn't standing up for her. Mary looked just fine. My eyes filled with tears. I had never witnessed such understanding and compassion for another being. Even this abrasive woman deserved to be heard. In the end she softened and murmured, "I know I shouldn't have hit a kid.

And I know Mary is just trying to teach her way, even if it's different from mine."

Later Gene talked about how, when we returned home from this retreat, we didn't have to defend Focusing. We weren't like the guy behind the complaints counter of a store, he said. We didn't have to stand up for the integrity of the product. It was better to just listen to how others felt.

At least once a year for the next few years I attended a week-long retreat at the Villa Redeemer. I came to have more and more respect for Mary McGuire. A particular time stands out in my mind of when it was my turn to be led through Focusing by her. I closed my eyes and turned my attention inwards.

Mary kept quiet. I waited and waited for her to come in with Clearing Space. Meanwhile, I was very busy inside, energy swirling through my upper body. I opened my eyes to see why she wasn't leading me through clearing a space.

Mary told me to stay with whatever was happening inside.

I paid attention to my body again. Everything within seemed to be reorganizing itself. My chest began to expand and I felt like the Michelin Man again. My lower body was becoming very solid. My lower spine was self-correcting, leaving my upper body free and fluid.

I could feel all the tension of my upper back. My right shoulder was so tight. Putting my attention into my right shoulder, I gave it permission to release.

Instead it cried out in anguish, "Can't you understand? I can't let go."

I was surprised. I didn't know this. It desperately wanted me to back off, to leave it alone.

Suddenly a little female appeared in the shoulder. The shoulder was like a cave. She hunkered down in the opening, afraid.

Down in my belly there was another voice. This one was impatient with my shoulder and just wanted me to get on with it. I paid attention to the voice and affirmed its wish to help in the situation. I acknowledged it was very powerful. It liked this and soon vanished.

I told the little female hunkered down in the opening of the cave that I would be back. I rolled a boulder to the mouth of the cave to protect her.

She was not very interested in whether I came back and didn't really expect me to be able to help.

When I reappeared at the cave she was surprised and suddenly hopeful. She left the cave, descended the hillside in a carefree spirit, and headed out to explore the sun and the air. Freedom, lack of fear! She was out of prison! She ran over the hills, joyful and free.

Everywhere was safe. She was free to explore anywhere in the body and anywhere outside.

At last I opened my eyes. Mary was still sitting with me, patient and smiling.

I had no idea what the small female would lead me to, but I knew it would be healing.

Chapter 12

Letters to My Parents

B esides my trips to Chicago, my sessions with Henry Regehr, my supervisor, and my personal therapy with Helen, I attended weekly group sessions with other beginning psychotherapists. In these groups we studied family theory by analyzing our own parent and sibling systems. I was fascinated by the dynamics of any family, and my own family was turning out to be more interesting than I would have liked. I was uncovering the dynamics of the couple who were my parents, discovering a sad, dysfunctional pair who were far from the ideal people I had created in my mind.

My journals from 1982 reveal that I continued working on my project to make sense of my family even when I went on vacation in July. As always we spent the time at our summer place on an island in Georgian Bay. Harvey was building a cottage to replace our big tent in the woods. Frank was thirteen years old, zipping around the bay in his aluminum boat, connecting with his friends. I was a woman who was involved in an intriguing, compelling search to figure out my own past.

Even in this idyllic setting I kept trying to make sense of the recent insights I had gleaned from my personal therapy and my professional development.

I was also busy earning my credentials as a marriage and family therapist. In the training sessions and my supervision sessions with Henry I was encouraged to ask my clients to write letters expressing their feelings—the sort of letters you don't mail.

That summer I wrote some letters myself—long, careful letters to both of my parents. My father had been dead for thirteen years. My mother was still alive and a part of my life. First I wrote to my mother.

July 20, 1982
Dear Mom:

I'm 44 years old this year—44 years since you were carrying me in your belly. I wonder how it was for you. How old were you? Younger than I am now.

You've often told me how Dad didn't want me. He was involved in the reserve army, in his Coke plant, and in his one beautiful four-year-old. Did you trick him into siring me? At any rate, I know he didn't want me and that he hurt you badly by ignoring you and by withdrawing from you. You've told me how your swelling shape repulsed him.

Your defence was to create a world which was yours and not his. You threw yourself into decorating your big, new house on the hill. Sublimation is healthy. I probably wouldn't have handled it as well. And you got angry at the bugger. As for me, I was yours—and that set the tone for our relationship. I was your thing, to use for whatever purposes you needed at the time. I wasn't even born yet and I had already lost my right to be whoever I needed to be.

And so I was born—to a mother who was angry and a father who was trying his darndest to ignore the impending birth. I wonder what prenatal influences I picked up.

My early years were marked by war breaking out and my father's disappearance into the army. That must have been terrible for you. You must have been distraught and distracted. This following a difficult birth and your doctor's orders not to hold me or lift me for the first three months of my life.

When I reflect on the circumstances of my first year of life I wonder how much of my present psychic malaise was planted then. I never really trust people to be there for me when I need them. When I'm in pain I withdraw into stillness and inertia. No amount of loving ever seems to fill up that emptiness inside me.

My earliest memory: You looking down at me. I'm six months old and I feel adorable, gurgling and cooing on a change table. Suddenly, I'm aware of your thoughts. I'm incredibly hurt. You're thinking, "She's red and fat and ugly. But she's mine and, dammit, I'm going to love her." For many years, I was angry with you for thinking this. Now I understand it somewhat differently. You were loving me in spite of your disappointment in my appearance. And that's at least acceptance. (I never have been able to accept myself or believe others accept me as okay.)

We're told these early memories are not factual. They're composite pictures, so to speak, reflecting the perception of one's experience.

I never trust my own perceptions. I thought I was adorable—a real charmer. You thought I was red, fat, and ugly. I always did look to you for the "correct version." These days I look to Harvey.

You left me when I was five and you had to go into hospital for surgery. You must have been very frightened, absorbed in your own aloneness and pain. You leaned heavily on your mother—and no wonder.

But before that—from the time I was a year old—you left me to run the Coke plant, to chase after your husband. So much for mother-child symbiosis in the first years.

I think I was five before I remember having you around. My main memories of those pre-school years are of Emma, the maid, who was scary, Grandpa's stiffness, and your mother's warm lap. No wonder I soaked up and luxuriated in my grandmother's caring. She was the only person in my life who cared primarily for me.

Those early years are filled with memories of fear and rejection and a sort of numb turning-off of my feelings and perceptions. After all, I got my strokes for never causing any trouble. It was very important not to upset you.

As I sit here thinking and remembering, I can't recall any happy memories from those years. Not one. Just fearful watchfulness.

A good memory just came to me—the Queens Hotel and hanging about the staircase. The man at the desk liked me. So did that travelling salesman. Dave Pinkney, who owned the hotel, made a fuss over me and took me out in his horse-drawn cutter that winter. Then we bought ice cream cones and giggled about ice cream on the coldest day of the winter. Then—a memory of rejection—he told me he liked my friend Dee better than me. That must have been an early Oedipal romance—and rejection.

By grades one and two, there was Dr. Gordon Greaves. I don't think my father was ever part of my Oedipal fantasies. I guess that's because he was never there. I guess, too, that explains my certainty I'd marry a doctor, like Dr. Greaves. You practically idolized doctors.

Dad came home when I was in grade two, the same year your mother died, and I lost the only person who thought I was wonderful. You tell me I'm "Daddy's girl" and that I look just like him. I have to accept your perception. There's an urgency to your statements. In retrospect, I realize it was my job to hold him in our family unit. He was making a decision—whether to return to England and the love of his life, or stay in Canada with us. I was yours and you used me as you needed me. My job was to keep him here. I succeeded. He felt strangled in his obligations as a result. That must have been terrible for you, never able to relax with him, always having to prove to him he'd made the right choice.

I got so fat from being passive and shutting off my feelings. You abhorred fat people. So why did you do it to me? Because eating kept me quiet and docile? So I wouldn't be too attractive to Dad? I was fat until I was able to take charge of my own nutrition. Being a fat kid was certainly devastating to my self image.

So we have birth to three months—never picked up. No bonding or symbiosis during the early years. Then, no Oedipal relationship with father who abandons us. The latency years—fat, not able to develop physical skills to take my place among peers. Instead I became a bossy, manipulative fat kid.

High school: Sociopathic boyfriend to whom I couldn't say "no." He and his crowd were too old for me—I did whatever he wanted. No pleasure in sexuality, just obedience, shutting down my feelings. Thinking of him now, I have a new perspective on him: There were some really nice aspects to him—his voice, his grin, his brightness, his singing. Later, I was so overwhelmed with guilt, I couldn't think about him without recoiling. But dammit, he was sensually pleasing in many ways. And he, like the rest of us, was making his way through life in the best way he knew how.

I guess I needed the reassurance of the steady relationship with him.

I still never openly rebelled, never learned to say "no" to you. I just split up my obedience between the two of you.

You chose my clothes. I looked to you for what to do and also what to think. We were very much together—maybe even "enmeshed"—in those days. Strange, considering our early lack of symbiosis.

Maybe if I'd had a chance to go through symbiosis and later "rapprochement," things would have been different. I guess I wasn't able to risk moving away from you far enough to become my own person.

Then came university. You were excited. You'd never gone. You were shaping me to be one of those bright, happy university types you'd admired but never been. You had a wonderful time buying my clothes—that was the essence of the experience. Books and mental preparation were incidental.

When we met in Toronto that September and October, you were hungry for details of my social successes. I was dating a future doctor [not Harvey] and that was promising. You thought I was absolutely cocksure, without any fears or uncertainties. And I was excited, too, about my social successes. I barely noticed the academic side of university.

Then I began to change. I wanted to be more serious—to delve into academic life. I was absorbing a new moral code and a new standard of values. A sense of shame for idle dilettantes, an appreciation for those who had had to work to come to university, a disdain for women who were here to find a good husband (the way I was).

You and I started clashing. Your eyes wandered in boredom as I talked of classes, professors, ideas. You involved yourself with me only when I talked about a party. I heard you desperately insisting, "No, you don't think that. You think ..." And then would follow *your* perception of the situation. You were losing your creation. I was getting away.

Then Harvey came along. We hung onto each other like two hungry mouths seeking sustenance and certainty. I know now that people choose mates at the same level of individuation as their own. I see now he was just as enmeshed with his mother as I was with mine. So we both traded enmeshments and clung to one another.

I probably could have had you as an ally in my wish to marry Harvey. But I made a tactical error. I went to my father asking for help—understanding so little of his jealousy for me.

Then came our real falling out. You took the wedding into your hands, ignoring our feelings. I had no part in it, Harvey backed out, and you were furious.

I became pregnant and told you. Harvey said I had to. That was a mistake. I was so passive through all of this. Yet nobody was looking out for me and everybody was angry with me.

Those were some of the worst days of my life. You were one of my biggest problems. For some reason, I felt obliged to hide my pain and fear from you. You were furious with me. I was violating everything you'd planned for me. No love came from you in those days—only anger and punishment. I decided to cut you off. I never again let you get close to me.

All those years you saw me as confident and unrepentant when I was really filled with fears and paralyzed by guilt.

Then Frank was born. Dad had died the previous summer. You needed me and moved in closer again. I listened to you and comforted you—but never shared anything of *my* feelings, of who I was. I just went through the motions of being with you. And when you'd leave, I'd either sigh with relief or sob out my anger and frustration with you.

You wanted Frank and you were willing to put up with Harvey and me to have him. I felt very tense with you—usually torn between you and Harvey—but you served my interests, too. Thanks to you, I had some breaks from mothering. I felt good leaving Frank with you, too. You were a strength in his life. His time with you was secure and loving. Poor little guy—his life with Harvey and me was often full of fights and bad feelings.

And now you're an old lady—and I'm getting older, too. And I still hide from you anything that doesn't fit your image of me. Maybe I should tell you someday, to explain some of my baffling arrogance, to be more real to you—or would that merely disappoint and confuse you?

Probably I couldn't get up the courage to violate your image of me, anyway.

So, you put up a front and I put up much more of one—two images nodding and talking to one another.

Love, Mary

Two days later, in my continuing struggle to understand my parents, I sat down and wrote to my father.

Georgian Bay. July 27, 1982
Dear Dad:

It's hard to sit down and write to you. I've put it off until the end of this peaceful day—and then nearly forgot this letter had been a priority for today. I find it hard to think about you, let alone write to you. I know you were not very interested in me when I was born. A year later you were gone—off to the war and more interesting pursuits than a wife and kids and a Coke plant. I know from Mom that you almost immediately regretted your decision. The discipline and discomfort were very hard on you—you softie. Nevertheless, several years later you were back, fit and trim.

You'd had many experiences away from us. What did we look like to you? I remember that you looked like a giant. I was fascinated by your power—and by your generosity. I remember attaching myself to your dressing gown hem and you were strong enough to pull me along the shiny floor. Your snores amazed me. Your toenails were intriguing. You laughed a lot at me. I seemed to surprise and bewilder you. You were gentle and attentive—yet I often feared the potential of your great strength.

I boasted to my friends about you. Mom told me constantly how powerful and important you were, and how aristocratic your family had been. She always presented an idealized version of you—no faults or weaknesses.

You seemed pleased with me. One of my best memories of you is when I was seven years old—tricking you into taking me on a camping holiday! That was very loving of you!

Throughout these years, I learned not to confront you too directly. A show of feeling was not to be tolerated. What a shy man you were—even with a little girl. How uneasy you were with your own emotions. It's hard to be with a child when your own emotions and opinions are not up front.

I remember when my grandmother died and you didn't come near me to comfort me. I had no idea you were also sad. When our friend Elly died, I told you of my sadness. You replied unemotionally, "If you believe in your religion, you'd say she's in heaven." I pressed you, looking for reassurance. Was Elly in heaven? You avoided my question.

How old were you in those days? About the age I am now?

The next time we went camping was when I was eleven and my sister's twins were born. There was no place for you in that house of women and sickly newborns. You drank heavily. You got sent away, and I was sent away, too, to look after you, while the women took care of the babies. My job was to keep you happy—in spite of the fact that my young life was endangered by your drunk driving.

Alcohol—did you drink because you couldn't say to my mother, "This is not what I want from life"? Did you kill your feelings and opinions with booze because you were in conflict with the reality of your life? Or couldn't you gain access to those feelings? Were they too far buried under prohibitions and "shoulds"?

In those days, I was often aware that you looked untidy. Your belly was often exposed—buttons popping with the weight you were gaining—or maybe just drunken disarray. I wonder about this. It must have been the reaction you elicited from others. I think people were repelled by you. I remember them smiling to hold you at a distance—not with respect. Probably you were on a manic high and reeking of rye whiskey. You were probably inappropriately friendly as well.

You weren't around much, otherwise—you worked long hours in the summer when Coke sales were up. And you drove around country roads in what you called your "kingdom," in your single man's Plymouth Coupe, looking for opportunities to increase the sale of Coke. I saw you as important and powerful. I accepted my mother's version of our family as socially superior— in spite of my father's shyness. The money you made was very important as proof of our social status as a family.

You did a lot of loud laughing with your friends. But did you have a real friend? Years later, I remember the affection your long-time employees had for you when you were sick and disabled. But where were your equals? Did Mom choose your social set?

High school: My chief value was as a sort of household jester to amuse you and keep you laughing.

I get a boyfriend. I'm messing up my life, but you stay distant from any emotional involvement. See no evil, hear no evil, speak no evil? I fail at school. You've always let me know you do not consider me very bright and do not expect much from me. My role is to amuse and to not cause trouble. All the signs are there that I am in trouble, but you choose to hide behind your newspaper. I guess what I was doing was pleading for you to involve yourself with me—to rescue me from self-destructiveness. I was humiliating myself and you let me. You didn't protect me.

I locked myself up in Bishop Strachan School, then managed to break out of my self-destructiveness and put the screws to you by sticking you with the second term's bill. That was good on my part. I broke the old patterns, managed to get myself out of "jail," and asserted my intention to run my own life. Good for me. I was taking responsibility for myself, since you wouldn't.

I came back home—my sister's new baby had been born and Mom was often in Winnipeg with my sister and the new baby. That was convenient for the family as I cooked and looked after you. The worst part of the job was that you chewed with your mouth open. This drove me wild, but I couldn't tell you and you wouldn't press for why I was upset.

When Mom came back, I was very jealous when she took over the house, replacing me so abruptly. Oedipal stuff? At seventeen?!

A year or so later, I often took pleasure in cutting her out of conversations you and I were having, deliberately steering the topic so she couldn't join in. You colluded. We often shut her out, you and I.

I was a sort of second wife all those years when you were sick.

Looking back, I see you as very selfish. You took my backrubs and my reading to you but you gave nothing in return. Even your conversation was something I sat through for *your* benefit. You felt good lecturing me on history. I listened—or looked as if I was listening—to please you.

I don't remember you ever expressing interest in what was happening in my life, except for amusing anecdotes. How could you have blinded yourself so totally to my reality and needs?

I remember hiding bad news from you. We all protected you from disturbing events. Was it a rationalization of our desperate need to keep the boat from rocking? To keep you with us?

When I went to Muskoka last weekend, it evoked memories of you which were warm and vibrant. I remembered your unbridled enthusiasm for Muskoka. I could just picture you driving along those winding roads, hooting with pleasure at the freedom, the delicious freedom of the country. You had a joy and bubbliness I've stamped out in myself. (I'm afraid of being like you?) I take myself so seriously.

You made a choice which was very different from mine. You chose to escape the challenge of a big company in Toronto for the affluent quiet of Stratford. It was the time of the Depression—but I wonder if you made the right choice. You made money, but you never felt proud of your work. The work you did feel proud of was done in your earliest days of civil engineering. You told me with pride how you had worked on the Welland Canal, designed a furnace, and so on.

It's just occurring to me as I write this that my mother always made a fuss about Coke being a great product. She was loyally joining you in your defection from the ranks of respectability. Perhaps she also felt guilty in being largely responsible for urging you to make money at the expense of social position. You told me your family back in Toronto was shocked that you had become a Coke bottler.

In Stratford, as Mom often said, you could be with the top of society, join the best (and only) country club, live in a big house, and entertain royally.

I think these were good days for you. You felt success-ful—you were making it. The photos of you in those days are filled with satisfaction and self-acceptance. I remem-ber particularly the pictures of you and Mom and my sister in Florida.

By the time I was on my way a couple of years later, your situation was evidently not happy. You didn't want another child. It sounds as if you didn't want the big house either. Was Mom pulling and shaping your life in ways you didn't want?

I understand you pretty well ignored my birth, that you were angry that I was on the way. Mom tells me you were repulsed by the size of her, too. You certainly didn't welcome me very warmly.

Then the war came and you had an excuse for extri-cating yourself from sticky domesticity. Mom told me you regretted the decision to enlist almost immediately. There followed several years of another kind of trap.

But this brings me to the point where this letter began—war-time—the time when the incongruity begins. I was excited, and scared, by you.

Mom always told me what to see. When you returned home, would it have been too hard to be honest about your uncertainty about life with us? I worked so hard to win you over!

Well, Dad, enough of this letter. I often think I feel your spirit in the seagulls—especially the ones that hover unusually close. I haven't felt you around on your birthday for a number of years, though. I do hope you are at rest. Go into the Light, Dad.

Love, Mary

My journal took on a different tone when I got back to the city in September. My dear friend Margaret was fifteen years older than I, a wise woman. She often offered me a different way of thinking about an issue. Here's what I wrote after confiding to her about my new perceptions of my parents.

Sept. 29, 1982
Dear Dad:
Consider this a P.S. to my letter in July.

I've just been talking with my friend Margaret—and only for a short time—but I had a real breakthrough in thinking about you.

I feel really angry with you. Damn you, anyway. You spent years yearning for a fantasy woman in England. So far as I can figure, you never saw her in all those years. But look what you did to your wife—kept her on tenterhooks all those years. You passive aggressively expressed your anger for her by secretly yearning for somebody else.

Damn you, anyway. I'm mad at Mom and also at myself. You made us feel so guilty and so insecure in holding onto you. Why couldn't you just have committed yourself and dug in? I guess that's why I always felt Mom was the one I could count on. At least she was committed. You really kept her dancing, trying to win you over.

Margaret said tonight, suppose he had gone off with the other woman—wouldn't he have set up the same patterns? Maybe you truly saved him from killing himself with guilt and anguish for leaving his family, she said.

The message for me: No wonder I revolt against being told I'm just like you. It's a good reminder to fully and wholeheartedly commit myself to my loving, caring mate.

You as a victim, Dad? Only as a victim of your own gutlessness. I'm really angry at what you did to us.

You could have had a very fine life if you'd thrown yourself into it and if you'd been clear on what you *did* want, not just what you did *not* want.

In hindsight I'm amazed I wrote those letters before my memories of childhood sexual abuse surfaced in my conscious mind. It would be almost two years before I found the underlying cause of my fears and depression.

PART III

Finding Lost Memories, Finding Myself

Chapter 13

Finding My Lost Memories

Christmas 1984. Two weeks of holiday. Two weeks with no work and no demands. Two weeks that ended up sweeping my past as I knew it out to sea, then tossing it back on shore in a different form. Each day of the holiday a tide of memory swept in, depositing new and disturbing scenes from my childhood. When the tide receded, it ebbed back out, taking with it the debris that hid my truth. What remained at the end of those two weeks was a beach swept clean of the fog and confusion of my early years. With the tangle of weeds and the mess of old, rotting branches gone, I could see more clearly. The "me" that got tossed up on the beach was the child sex object of her father and of his father, my proper old grandfather.

I didn't want to be a survivor of child sexual abuse. In my work as a psychotherapist I was steadfastly respectful and supportive while my clients grappled with the sad reality that the adults they depended on had betrayed them. Over time I would try to help these brave souls deal with the shame of being a sex object, a crime for which children inevitably blame themselves.

When my own memories of childhood sexual abuse started surfacing I was no different from my clients. I struggled against the shocking new history I was being forced to accept. I almost hoped I was confusing my own past with that of my clients. Vicarious traumatization is a phenomenon well-recognized by professionals who work with people who have suffered terrible traumas. Could I be confusing my professional work with my personal life? Were these my memories or a mélange of my clients' recollections?

That Christmas Harvey and I decided to stay home to pay attention to our inner lives. Our work with our clients' trauma and dissociation had pretty well worn us out. We had no energy to invest in family, friends, or the holy season. Burned out and exhausted we agreed to spend the holiday Focusing and journaling together.

One morning during that vacation I awoke knowing my sleep had been disturbed by bad dreams. With no pressure to jump out of bed I propped myself up on my pillows and concentrated on how my body carried the unconscious activity of the sleep state.

"How am I feeling in my body?" I asked myself. A queasy, uneasy sense of revulsion stirred in my abdomen. I stayed with it, allowing the vague discomfort to sharpen around the edges. At last a visual image of a black worm formed itself out of the physical sensation. Unsettling. Not something I wanted to entertain. Yet I knew from my training to stay with it. The black worm looked at me. I shuddered. It had some sort of power over me—frightening power. A repulsive, irresistible force pulled me into it.

I gave the dream creature the name Black Worm so I would remember it.

After the holiday I took the experience to Helen, my therapist. As she had advised me to do with that other scary creature, Gollum, she said, "Make friends with it."

Wormie, like his predecessor, scared me, but heeding Helen's advice I spent time each day paying attention to the body sensation and the visual image of Wormie. I talked with Wormie and honestly tried to make friends with the repulsive little creature. No luck. I continued to stay with the bodily felt sense of this strange creature.

Then one morning I awoke with the clear knowledge that Wormie was Grandpa's penis. There was no way I was going to make friends with Wormie and accept him as a part of myself. Wormie did not belong inside me. He was definitely not a part of me I needed to own. With this knowledge came the realization that my grandfather had sexually abused me until I was seven, when the war ended and my father returned home. The thought bubbled up and settled in my brain, plain and clear.

All at once I was privy to my own history. Life began to make sense. No wonder I'd had trouble in so many areas of my life.

I told Harvey about my recent epiphanies involving my grandfather. He looked at me and said, "At least your father didn't sexually abuse you." As he said this I was startled by another new certainty. Again I instantly knew beyond a doubt that my father as well as my father's father had used me sexually.

"Yes he did," I replied, amazed at this revelation. My story was beginning to tell itself without my prompting.

It certainly wasn't a straightforward healing and recovery from child sexual abuse. I still had doubts. Maybe I was just making this up to explain my failings. Maybe I was making excuses for my inadequacies.

On the one hand I was pushed forward by wanting to

know the truth that would set me free. On the other hand I was pulled back into amnesia by the embarrassment of what I was uncovering.

All during that holiday I continued to journal, to chart my inner life, and to be open to whatever dreams, thoughts, feelings, and knowing bubbled up to the surface of my awareness. Here are some excerpts from those journal entries:

Dec. 27, 1984
12.15 a.m. — Went to sleep at 10. Wakened, heart pounding; dream of hearing a woman talking with much emotional intensity about complications of going on a trip. Shipboard supper—and we need our juniper cocktails. I'm picking up the underlying hysteria of the conversation, assuming she must be talking about something that makes a lot of sense to her. Something that covers up the real pain of her life. The way my mother's friends talk.

Half asleep, I prop myself up in bed to Focus on the dream. There's a bodily sense of prickliness on the surface of my belly. Then a visual image of an old rusting screen with a hole in it. It's the screen on my grandfather's bedroom window in our old house.

There's a sense of his smell, pipe tobacco and old man's dry skin. Up close, his wine coloured smoking jacket with the black piping.

I'm on Grandpa's lap, back to him, leaning on him, held tight against him. He's stimulating my clitoris, my eroticism. When he's finished, he chides me for liking what we've just done—his scorn for me after I've gone through this confusing, delicious sensation of sexuality.

Confusion! For child—grandfather's actions—what happens between us; my mother's friend in the dream is hysterical, too, although I can't understand just why, something about juniper cocktails.

2:45 a.m. — I waken again. Mother's young face angry—rage directed at me. "You're a nasty little girl!"— i.e., I deserve to suffer. I tell the little girl, no matter what you've done, I'll stay with you and love you.

Dec. 29

Little girl experiencing eroticism. Last night before sleeping, recalling earlier surfaced memory of sitting on Grandpa's lap and having his boney finger stimulate me to orgasm.

Wakened this a.m. with a sense of sadness and badness. The sick, heavy feeling in my diaphragm. It was about being in Grandpa's bedroom, early spring eve, air outside is soft and sensuous; the gentle boughs of the fir trees outside the open window.

Grandpa is saying almost distractedly, "Come here, child." He's getting something out of a white linen handkerchief. I don't know what it is. Later, I figure out it's a tube of Vaseline. He lays me crosswise on the bed—my orgiastic response to his actions.

Dec. 31

Most days I waken filled with sadness. Harvey said yesterday that my grandfather robbed me of my childhood. I'm only beginning to realize how much was taken from me. I hate waking with an achy head and tired eyes.

Propped up in bed before I'm really awake. A picture of myself at age seven pops into my mind. I'm sitting on a rock at the back of our house. Rolls of fat circle my middle. I'm an ugly blob of a kid—no feelings inside her, she's dead inside. I've never liked that little girl.

Jan. 2, 1985
Focusing with Harvey. He asks me: "How does your body
feel about these memories surfacing?"

A shaking, quaking in my diaphragm. Like a membrane
which has sealed the tightly layered memories. A Vesuvius
of memories exploding. Mother will be angry with me for
upsetting the accepted view of the family.

A memory of being very small on Grandpa's lap. I'm in
a fantasy, pretending as I roll around with my body, one leg
up, legs apart, or something. Suddenly it becomes something dirty and shameful. Grandpa turns it into something
sexual, hands on my genitals. I'm shocked, feel I've done
something wrong. I didn't know it was bad or that it would
lead to something bad.

I promise to myself to be very careful, not to play and be
carefree—and never to relax when somebody's around.

The following journal entries are dated three years later. Now
that I knew the underlying cause of my lifelong emotional distress, and now that I'd "birthed" my lost memories, I'd hoped
for a release from the heavy, dark shadow that had always hung
over me. That release wouldn't come for some years, as my
journal notes from that period reveal. There were still strange
dreams and more memories that made me really angry. In fact
anger was the dominant emotion of these years.

Jan. 6, 1987
I waken very slowly, still in my dream state. I'm dancing with
Grandpa. I'm very small. There's a tickling sensation in my
lower abdomen. It's close to eroticism. Grandpa holds me
in his arms. His music box plays pretty music. The feeling
is becoming orgasmic. Then I'm on his lap. We're sitting in

his big green armchair. I see his penis. It's black with sparse black hairs sprouting along the length of it. It's Wormie!

With that, I'm fully awake!

I think of how I've always avoided dancing. I'm practically phobic about social dancing—always dreaded being asked to get out on the dance floor. Harvey's the only man I'm comfortable dancing with. Without realizing why, I've always told myself I don't want to dance with any man I wouldn't have sex with.

Jan. 7
Focusing with Harvey. Terrible experience for me. Left me full of frustration and rage. Here I am at midnight as I write this, realizing why. I was into the possible abuse by my grandfather, body moving all over, face full of pain, breathing indicating I was into something very deep. Harvey was doing something that had nothing to do with my experience.

"Can you find a handle for that?" he asks while I'm writhing with the experience of a huge hand holding me down by the solar plexus.

The experience was very hard to hold onto; very fragile—and he was just blabbing on cheerfully, totally insensitive to my pain. I didn't realize until I was in bed why—he had his eyes closed! He was paying attention to his own felt sense. He was oblivious to me.

This makes me not want to Focus with him again—which, of course, is not what I want either. I have to talk to him.

Jan. 8
I sat down with Harvey to tell him how awful it felt to have him be insensitive to my pain, preoccupied with his own agenda, brightly chattering while I was suffering.

He tells me he closed his eyes because he can't stand to watch me do all that grotesque stuff—jaw clicking, etc. Then he recalled that it reminded him of his drunken mother whose head would fall to the kitchen table following her jaw clicking.

Jan. 9

I decided to risk Focusing with Harvey again. He went first and had some good insights. When it was my turn, I was nauseated from my throat to my stomach. A long sausage shape filled this space. My mean voice came in to say, "Oh yeah, sure, make it like every survivor's imagery. A sausage."

I ignore the mean voice's scepticism. The handle is now "scraped raw." This brings a shift, especially in my belly.

Flash to the Queens Hotel where we lived in the winter— me at five years old, outside building a snowman. Adults pass by and smile, but don't engage. Nobody really cares what I'm doing—they're just going through the motions. Nobody really wants to get involved with me.

Flash to our rooms in the hotel, mother busy, grand-father reading in his chair.

Little girl is full of rage. Mother won't hear the awful things Grandpa is doing to her. She just chatters on brightly, not really engaging. Little girl has been trying to tell her. Can't let herself feel the rage, either. Rage is about being used.

"You're supposed to be looking after me [while mother is at work, running the Coke plant] and you're getting the gratification," I tell him [my grandfather] in my Focusing session.

Harvey suggested I assure the little girl I'll be with her

and accept whatever she tells me. I should try to ease her loneliness. "What did Grandpa do?" he asks.

The little girl describes sitting on his lap, her back to him. He's reading to her. Then she turns and notices to her horror his penis is out on his lap. He rubs it against her buttocks. She is paralyzed with fear and disgust.

Then there's a scene where she faces him and he puts his penis between her thighs, holding her thighs together. I assure the little girl she's not bad.

All of this fits with my body shifts and my life experience. If I were my own client, I wouldn't have a bit of doubt. Some part of me, though, wants so badly to dismiss it as imagination and hysteria.

"It couldn't happen in my family." I am hit with an overwhelming sense of disloyalty. I imagine my mother's horror and anger with me for saying such a thing. I'm having all the reactions my client survivors have. It will be very strange to break the silence. Where to start?

By the next night, Sunday, I was reeling with all these memories. Looking at my journal I realize how hard I was struggling with my denial. I wanted to heal. If it were child sexual abuse that was making my life difficult then I wanted to get on with accepting and healing. On the other hand if I were just making all this up, I'd better be careful.

Jan. 10
How do I feel about all these newly accessed memories? I Focus on the question. A heavy, black bowling ball in my stomach, a white circle with an eight drawn on it. "I'm behind the eight ball." Fear in my buttocks.

"I'm in real trouble now." Flashback to child on toilet at

Queens Hotel. Vagina is sore and scraped. Grandpa was trying to get his penis inside it. Little girl is terrified her mother will find out because mother would be really mad at her for getting hurt this way. I comfort the little girl and imagine putting white, cool ointment on her burning vagina.

She says, "It's a dirty, bad place." I say no—no place in your body is bad or dirty. And you're not bad. It's Grandpa who's bad. I tell her we'll talk again soon.

Funny how I'm not really believing this. I keep thinking maybe I'm making it all up—better be careful and not disclose. Then I'll be stuck with this version of my own history.

Jan. 13

I awoke three nights in a row bathed in sweat. I was in my grandfather's old bedroom at the top of the stairs on John St. Something about bumping down every step of the long staircase, intentionally spanking my behind on the stairs.

A pressing-down feeling just at the base of the throat in my upper chest. "Holding me down" on Grandpa's lap, head near his knees. His dinner napkin under my bottom. His penis pushing against my vagina. He's angry because he can't come. He pushes and pushes at me, muttering "damn."

Once they started, the memories rolled over me like waves in the ocean. I could no more stop them than I could keep breakers from smashing up on the shore.

I didn't want to have been sexually abused. I wanted to be the girl from the respectable family whose father adored her and whose old grandfather cared enough to take her on his weekly walks to the library. I treasured the stories of my camping trips with my father. I wanted the father who laughed at my jokes and told me I would one day take over his Coca-Cola plant.

I wanted a nice family. I wanted to be a normal, healthy woman, not a trauma victim. What I was remembering was shameful. My head knew *I* hadn't done anything bad. I'd been a helpless child. Still, I was tortured by shame. I felt dirty. I held a secret, a secret so terrible I'd kept it from myself all these years.

And why had the memories come now? My life was better than it had ever been. I'd finished my graduate studies and set up a private practice. I was connected with a caring group of psychological mentors who were training me in Focusing. My relationship with Harvey was tender and supportive. Frank, our son, was a healthy, handsome eighteen-year-old. Why now?

Yet I knew from my professional work that memories of trauma tend to lurk hidden in the unconscious until we're strong enough to handle them. Forty is a common age for recovering lost memories. Until I was ready to handle them the sickening memories lay in wait. Denial protected me from what I couldn't face. In retrospect there were plenty of signs that the memories were just on hold until I was strong enough to let them surface.

It was a gut-wrenching period in my life. For two years I was self-absorbed, lost in ugly reveries of childhood truths. With each new memory of sexual abuse I felt better and worse. Better because life made more sense. Worse because I was forced to give up another chunk of my personal history. I was not who I thought I was.

A heavy gray rock weighed down my chest and stomach. Sleep brought frightening nightmares. Sometimes the scenes were from my clients' lives and sometimes from my own. What a terrible world we live in, where adults use defenceless children for their sexual gratification. Organized rings of pedophiles terrify their child victims into forgetting they've been gang raped. Pornographers with their bright lights and cameras photograph children having sex with adults. The children are forced to smile for the camera and say they like being raped. Usually the children don't remember. They are too frozen in fear to be able to report their perpetrators. Knowing all this I wasn't sure some days I wanted to live in such a world.

I had all the signs of depression. My sleep was disturbed, food didn't interest me, and it was hard for me to concentrate on what I was reading. Nothing really grabbed my interest. My body was heavy, weighing me down with its lack of energy. Sex was just a bother. I avoided other people as it was too much effort to be with them.

I noticed I was also becoming somewhat paranoid. When I got in the elevator at work, travelling to my office on the ninth floor, I would stiffen, wondering which of the men in business suits could be child sexual predators. I knew from my own experience and from my clients' stories that men who abuse children don't wear horns. They are often respected figures in their communities.

I had no proof I'd been sexually abused as a child, only my own knowing. How I wished someone would come forward from my past and tell me they had walked in on a scene of my father or my grandfather having sex with me. Maybe some other person who had been a child the same time that I was would tell me my father had abused them. I could think of several such possibilities. Alas, I had nothing but a jigsaw puzzle with some missing pieces.

So much made sense at last. No wonder I hadn't been able to pay attention in school when I was a child! I now understood why, as a young adult woman, I didn't mourn my father's death. Once when my mother was visiting my house she mistook some mail about child pornography as something sent for Harvey's entertainment. She laughed! She thought that was fine. Thinking back I'm reminded of the whole of society laughing during *Annie Get Your Gun* when pregnant Annie tells the audience she's just a girl who can't say no. Wait a minute! That was me! I, too, couldn't say no.

If I accepted my history of child sexual abuse it would explain the mysteries of much of my life. Why was I so anxious about meeting some nameless person whenever I left our house? I was particularly phobic about seeing anyone from Stratford. Unconscious shame would explain that, especially with people from there. Otherwise it made no sense at all.

I'd always had a strange relationship with cupboards, closets, and drawers. Years went by when I never really emptied or tidied them. I just threw more things in and shut them fast before ... before what? Once my memories surfaced I noticed a change in my behaviour. I began clearing out cupboards, closets, and drawers. Some survival part of my brain realized these dark places held no danger. No monsters were going to jump out at me from their hidden depths.

The more I was able to accept what I didn't want to accept, the more I could be with myself in a caring, compassionate way. If I could just get past the pathetic, wounded self-image I could get on with my healing. I certainly wouldn't have been hard on anyone else who was struggling to accept her past. I was constantly telling my clients they were not to blame, not responsible, for the sex acts that took place when they were children. I told them they had nothing to fear from the past.

At last I knew why I was often sad. Before my memories surfaced I was relieved when I had some normal, sad event to relate to. People could understand that. They couldn't appreciate my inexplicable depressed states. And I finally realized why I never let myself fully experience joy. If I were truly happy, something bad would follow. If I let down my guard and relaxed, something threatening was sure to happen. Faced with any stress my emotions ranged from fear and anxiety to numbness and a lack of feeling, with nothing in between.

It's uncomfortable to have someone notice that you startle at the slightest unexpected noise or movement. It is much more embarrassing, however, to act out your traumatized brain's exaggerated response to every situation it perceives as threatening. Benign events can easily be misinterpreted by the traumatized brain as life-threatening.

When I was in my mid-thirties, taken up with teaching yoga and caring for my little son, I needed extensive treatment for gingivitis. For hours on end I lay back in a chair, helplessly undergoing whatever the periodontist cared to do to me. One day, after a particularly painful session, my periodontist moaned, "I need a rest."

I reached my hand up to hold his arm. "Oh no," I said, "you need a nice yoga teacher."

There was a long quiet pause. I was barely aware of how out-of-keeping my gesture and words had been—until I went home and came back to my senses. What had I said? I was so embarrassed! Where had those words come from? Clearly, being helpless in the chair while he hurt me convinced my traumatized self I was in a sexual situation with no option but to cooperate in the hope of getting out of there alive.

Dr. Bessel A. van der Kolk, a clinician, researcher, and teacher specializing in post-traumatic stress, has suggested that women throughout history have submitted to conquerors in a response designed to perpetuate the species. I don't know whether this is true. I do know, though, that I reacted in a manner entirely incongruous with my normal personality.

My next appointment was a short one so I took our five-year-old son with me. Of course the periodontist wanted to meet him. Frank was a sturdy, handsome child with big blue eyes and curly blond hair.

"He's a good looking kid," the periodontist said to me. "Look at the build on him! Wow!"

I took the opportunity to say, "He's built like his father. His father's a very handsome man."

Meanwhile, our family dentist told my husband he should have his gums checked by the same periodontist. My husband was not sure why, but went anyway, on the advice of our dentist. Of course there was nothing wrong with my husband's gums. Apparently my "seduction" had proved interesting to the periodontist, who followed up by wanting a look at my husband. My humiliation grew. I did what I could to restore his impression of me as a happily married woman and cringed every time he said, "Myrtle and I ..." in reference to his wife, as if he needed to protect himself from further advances.

A couple of times, years later, I was triggered into trauma by Eugene Gendlin. Scaring me was the last thing the poor man had on his mind. The first occasion was in a Focusing training session in Chicago. We were all seated in a large circle. Gene was talking about Japanese temple guards, fierce statues meant to keep the temple safe from evil spirits. I think he was comparing our own defence mechanisms to temple guards. He contorted his face and pulled his arms up into the position of threatening paws. He lunged across the circle at me to demonstrate. I completely lost awareness of the present benign context and found myself huddled into a terrified ball on my chair. When at last I came to I looked around at the circle.

Nobody seemed to have noticed. Maybe they thought I was just a good actress.

Another time I was leading a retreat at Niagara Falls. The setting was an old stone convent overlooking the falls, a former Roman Catholic school for girls. My room was the former mother superior's old room, and it adjoined another fine room, both of which overlooked the falls. A shared bathroom separated the two spacious rooms.

Gene Gendlin was the guest teacher. I had put him in the adjoining room. He said he loved the view of the falls and was enjoying the wonderful old convent that housed us.

"Let me see your room," he said as we were returning to the bedroom floor. He followed me into my room.

The next thing I knew I'd jumped into the spacious clothes closet. How did I get there? I do not know. Some primitive part of my brain reacted in terror to the present harmless situation. I was like the traumatized war veteran diving under the table when a car backfired outside. There was no time to think. My survival mechanism was triggered and I reacted without consciously registering any danger. It was a remarkable albeit humiliating demonstration of how the traumatized brain can react to a perceived threat.

Once I regained my senses, I followed Gene to his room, trying to look as if nothing unusual had happened. I have no idea what he thought of my sudden disappearance.

Can you imagine how I beat myself up before I was able to make sense of these embarrassing events? In all three instances I was humiliated. But once I had accessed my memories I could be compassionate with myself. I knew why I had behaved so strangely with both of these harmless men who had set off my primitive brain's survival responses.

My primitive brain perceived the dentist as a perpetrator for whom I experienced tender, loving thoughts. He was hurting me. I was helpless. During the long appointment when I behaved seductively, he had inadvertently punctured my sinus. He was worried. I reassured him it was nothing to worry about.

How crazy all this seems to the adult, rational brain. Yet while I was lying back in his chair I wanted only to comfort him and take care of him. I did not matter. My suffering was inconsequential. That is exactly how I felt as a child with my father.

As for Gene, he is a man whom I admire enormously. I even love him for his compassion and for his ability to share his rare intelligence. A father figure? Certainly a mentor and someone who changed my life for the better. Maybe a grandfather whose wisdom and knowledge begat so many beautiful offspring.

The woman who jumped into the closet is the same woman who organized the retreats at Niagara Falls. I spent years building a teaching centre where I trained and taught both professionals and lay people to bring out the wisdom in themselves and others through Focusing.

My own maturity and my ability to help people drew scores of participants to the retreats. Over the years I carefully chose and mentored my teachers, organizing the days for practice, free time, meal time, and social time. Best of all, it worked. And this was not by chance. My Centre for Focusing in Toronto was the most successful Focusing centre in North America—maybe in the world.

Survivors experience a huge split in their personalities. In some situations they may be the person they would have been without the wounding. They have whatever skills and abilities are theirs by birth and effort. But the wounded part will also respond to unexpected and seemingly harmless triggers. The wounded part knows nothing about the adult's secure position in the world. Unless it is educated about itself and nurtured through a long healing process, it can remain forever terrified and helpless.

The emotional brain responds and acts so fast that the thinking brain doesn't even know what's happening. We still have the limbic brain of our primitive ancestors. The cells of the body hold the memory of past danger. Our brains are meant to ensure the preservation of our species. Even in the twenty-first century, when the limbic brain decides we are threatened by a danger that is inescapable and intolerable, it takes over to ensure we act without thinking in order to survive. Its way of ensuring our continued existence may not fit with our modern age, for the primitive brain knows only about primitive responses.

Chapter 14

Going Deeper

The memories kept coming. I remembered how, when my father was overseas during the war and my mother was running the Coke plant, Grandpa was left in charge of me. A live-in housekeeper and couple of girls from the country helped out. Grandpa made them happy by allowing them generous time off. This was when he introduced me to the strange finger-rubbing world of Vaseline and overwhelming bodily sensations. We would dance together, Grandpa and I, to the tinkling sounds of his antique music box. Then, hand-in-hand, Grandpa limping and cursing his goddamned painful knees and hips, we'd climb the stairs to his bedroom.

It was something we never told anybody. It was always the same. It started when I was a few years old. I would lie on Grandpa's bed as he opened the cigar box on his table and took out the white handkerchief wrapped around the tube of Vaseline. Slowly and carefully, he would cover the end of his index finger.

Then, sitting on the edge of the bed, he would pull down my underpants and rub my pee-pee so that that my whole body was filled with the most overpowering waves of pleasure. Sometimes it was too much and felt like the time I stuck a bobby pin in an electric socket and didn't know what hit me. While I was caught up in the labyrinth of sensations he would unzip his fly and take care of himself, then wipe himself with the white handkerchief.

Once I had a good look at his snake-thing. It was dark with scraggly hairs sticking out everywhere.

I soon learned that our little secret gave me power. I could demand candy for sex. My old Grandpa, leaning on his cane and cursing his arthritis every step of the way, would hobble off to the corner store at my command.

I remember my mother scolding him for buying me so much candy.

"Peg," he said to her, "you can't imagine how she pesters and pesters me. I don't get any peace until I get her some."

It never occurred to my mother that my grandfather and my father had sex with me. It's not that she wasn't vigilant about my sexual activities when I was a girl. She fussed a lot about my sexuality, but always at the wrong times.

Robby, my constant playmate, lived across the street from our house. Behind his house the lawns flowed one into the other with no fences to obstruct children's activities. Back porches offered a view of this grassy playground. Beyond the green lawns the communal gardens stretched down towards the river.

On the particular summer day I remember, Robby and I were busy with our three-year-old exploration of all the wonders offered by a dozen back yards. Behind one house we found a collection of empty flower pots. We weren't sure what to do with them once we had piled them up and arranged them in a circle.

Robby had an idea. He pulled down his tartan shorts and showed me how he could pee into the flower pots standing up. I was amazed. Looking at his fleshy equipment I couldn't have been more delighted if he'd shown me a newborn puppy. I followed by demonstrating for him how I had to squat over the flower pot. We were both pleased with our new discoveries and went on to the morning's next adventure.

When it was time to go home Robby's nursemaid came to walk me across the street to my house. I sensed something was very wrong the moment I entered our front hall. My mother was nowhere to be seen. Usually she greeted me at the door to tell me to wash my hands before I touched anything.

At last I found her in her second-floor bedroom, sewing. She didn't look up at me. I stood confused, wondering what was going on. Finally she spoke:

"You're a very bad, nasty girl," she snapped.

"I didn't do anything," I managed to mutter, having no idea what my sin had been.

Never looking me in the eye, she took me by the shoulders to her full length mirror and turned me so I could see my back. My skirt was caught up in my panties. I remembered the flower pots. Was that a bad thing? She told me a neighbour whose back porch looked out on the green lawns had seen Robby and me peeing in the flower pots and had phoned my mother. Still burning with anger and disgust she sent me off to wash my hands thoroughly. I had no defence. The skirt proved my badness.

Another time comes to mind. This event took place in our tall, narrow downstairs washroom, the one that was just inside the front door.

I was seven and it was my birthday. Charron, my best friend, and I had organized a little kids' playtime during the summer months. We would round up the younger children in the neighbourhood and entertain them with a couple of hours of games. I really liked these smaller children. My mother offered me a separate party just for them.

It was during this party that Charron and I went into the washroom together. We were feeling very grown up and were telling each other stories about the little kids. Suddenly the door ripped open to reveal my furious mother, angry and disgusted because we were doing something very dirty in there.

No amount of denial or explaining could convince her otherwise. To this day I don't know what she thought we were doing. I think she always knew, unconsciously, that there was something disgusting, disturbing, and sexual about me. I only wish she'd been more vigilant when it may have helped me.

It was the summer after the war ended. My mother rented a cottage at Port Albert, Ontario. My father was driving around in his single man's car, the Plymouth Coupe. My mother was furious at him for buying a non-family car. He was being passively aggressive about her cottage rental. She'd rented a humble dwelling—a five-minute walk from the beach—without consulting him. He would arrive at the shabby cottage, complain it was a dump, and refuse to spend the night in such a place. Then he'd disappear for a few more days.

We got to know the owners of the cottage next door, a year-round two-storey white house with black trim. This was the G. family. I think they had three children: an older sister, a brother, and a younger brother. I don't remember much about that summer, but I do recall that my mother's Buick sat in front of the cottage and that it became the setting for youthful experimentation with sex. The older boy claimed the front seat for his adventures with a girl. The little brother and his girlfriend took the back seat. Apparently my mother and the other adults knew nothing of the steamy sex play of these children ranging in ages from eight to thirteen.

I was excluded from the activities in the Buick until one day when the backseat "girlfriend" had gone travelling with her grandmother. I was invited to join the little brother on the floor of the car, under the blanket. I was pleased to be included but unimpressed with what followed. I felt his hand on my private parts. Why was he doing that? What did they get out of it? I felt nothing except bewilderment. He placed my hand on his penis. I knew this had to be wrong.

That was my last time under the blanket. I had no wish to return.

⁂

Sometimes I question my memory. Is my memory of early childhood selective, recalling only trauma, fear, and sexual abuse? Maybe there were times when my mother enjoyed the little person I was. Sadly, only one time of her being really nice to me stands out in my memory. Why, I wonder, would such an ordinary event be memorable?

I was about four years old and wearing wet rubber boots. I was standing at the front door of our huge white house, wanting to come in. My mother brought over a chair and ordered me to sit on it until she returned. She smiled at me in a friendly way and lifted me onto the chair.

"Now don't move until I come back." She disappeared up the curving staircase, her hand on the polished banister I liked to slide down. I sat there by the grandfather clock.

"Would you know if I moved?" I called after her.

She turned around and looked at me curiously.

"Yes, I'll know."

I was left to ponder how this was possible. The black tile floor gleamed. Oh, I'd probably leave wet boot marks, I thought.

That's all I remember—just that she was really nice to me.

When it came time for me to date boys, my mother worried a lot. But she always worried at the wrong time. There were times she should have been worried, but those smooth-talking boys aroused no suspicion. Years later, when I first opened my private practice for marital counselling, she hurt me deeply by saying I would probably get the unmarried couples that respectable agencies refused to see. Somehow my couples work struck her as dirty and demeaning. I was sad about her disrespect for my chosen career. I hadn't yet grasped that she knew, unconsciously, there *was* something odd about me and sex.

So many events made sense now I had my memories—like the one about our family doctor, Harold Kenner. He gained my trust and respect one afternoon when I was seven. By now my father had returned from the war. It was a period in my life when my father and my grandfather seemed to have had a tacit agreement about who got to have sex with me. Whatever passed between the two men, my grandfather no longer took me to his bedroom at the top of the stairs. I could not hide from my younger, more agile father. I belonged to him now. Besides, it was my job to keep him from going back to England and leaving us again. I had to make him happy to be with us.

One afternoon when I was seven my mother dropped me off at the Kenners' house. Mrs. Kenner had offered to keep an eye on me for the afternoon. The Kenners were good friends with my family. Mary, their daughter, was always nice to me, in spite of her being my sister's friend. I was playing with a fluffy stuffed dog belonging to Mary, totally caught up in a game of fantasy. There I was in a second-floor bedroom of their large house, far away from any route of escape, when suddenly I realized Dr. Kenner was standing right beside me.

"Hello, Mary Kay," he was saying. I could hear him, but I couldn't move. I was paralyzed with terror. I was also mad at myself for being stupid enough to let down my guard and relax and play. My heart pounded and everything went to fuzz in my head. At long last he left the room and I just stood there frozen. When I was once again able to think and feel I felt confused. How come he hadn't done anything like my father and my grandfather did when they found me alone?

I wonder what the experience was like for Dr. Kenner. In the safety of his office with his ever-present nurse I was relaxed and friendly, but not in his home alone. I liked him, too, when our families got together. Did he see my terror? Did he wonder why I froze? Maybe he never thought about it again. Maybe he simply thought I was a strange little kid. It probably never occurred to him to wonder about child sexual abuse. Nobody wondered about sex with children in those days. It didn't happen.

My worst memory is of one Christmas when my father came home on leave from the war. I was sitting with him beside the beautiful Christmas tree. It was loaded down with presents and glowing with tree lights. Daddy took me on his knee and started hugging and kissing me. He told me how much he loved me and how pretty I was with my blonde hair and blue eyes. I was his little princess.

He started kissing me hard, on the lips. I felt his hand go under my underpants, to the same place Grandpa's fingers went. I knew what was coming, the sense of my small body being helplessly overwhelmed as his fingers played with my pee-pee. Soon I was peeing rainbows and summer rain. I drifted into a magic sea of orgiastic ecstasy, barely aware of the white stuff shooting out of his penis onto my bare tummy.

When he let out a huge moan and his body slumped I got scared. What was wrong with my Daddy? He must be sick, like when people threw up.

The next moment I was scared for me, not for him. His eyes, big and blue like mine, looked into my face and he told me that if I ever told anyone what we'd just done, he would have to kill me. His hands were on my throat. Just to make sure I understood what "kill" meant, he pressed on my windpipe until I began to lose consciousness. He'd be very, very sad if he had to kill me, so he hoped I would never, never tell anyone.

How is it that I could have so completely forgotten these terrors? I guess my child's brain did what it had to do so I could survive. There was no way to escape. There was nobody I could tell. I'd probably have gone crazy if I hadn't forgotten.

I have written the following from my imagination. It must have gone something like this when I was a child:

The tinkle of ice cubes in my father's glass flicks a switch in my brain. It happens so fast I don't even register I've heard him coming. He's still in the downstairs hall. Now he's climbing the staircase. I, me, Mary Kay, jump under my high four-poster bed.

I barely feel Daddy's hands grab my shoulders to hug me and tell me how much he loves me. My body is already dividing in two. Mary Kay stays under the bed giggling and having fun with Daisy and Donald.

Donald Duck and Daisy Duck welcome me into their world with the familiar cartoon music. "Quack, quack, Donald Duck," I greet him, laughing. "Quack, Daisy." It's so much fun being with them.

It's the other girl who hugs Daddy. Her name is Sally. I know Daddy's holding her tight, telling her she's his little princess.

I can tell he's rubbing her between her legs. He's telling her that his Horsey wants to nibble her sugar cubes. He's rubbing his Horsey on her funny spot until Horsey gets big and swollen. Then he'll want her to hold Horsey tight until it gets big enough to throw up all over her legs and tummy.

Sally does anything he says. She cuddles Daddy and lets his big fingers send those weird funny tingles flooding through her like the tide I saw rushing in when we went to Florida. I watch her groan like she's in pain when all the tingles explode inside her. She looks really stupid, mouth open, half crying, half laughing, "Oh Daddy, oh Daddy!"

Sally is very, very bad. She's also really beautiful. She's not a little blonde girl like me. Sally's got big brown eyes and short, curly brown hair.

Mommy often blames me for things Sally does. Like the time Mommy's favourite vase got broken. I told Mommy that Sally broke it, but she didn't believe me. She still thought I'd done it. It's not fair.

I actually had a big doll that looked just like Sally. I called her Sally, too. One day I was playing with her at my grandmother's apartment. My mother and my grandmother were there in the living room, talking.

All of a sudden I got so mad at Sally, I thought I'd burst. I wanted to kill her! I was shaking her and screaming at her. I pulled off both her arms and was trying to pull off her legs. I bashed her head on the carpet, holding onto one of her legs.

I became aware of my mother grabbing me. Both women stared, horrified. "Darling, darling," my mother said, trying to calm me. I looked down at my beautiful doll, ruined forever.

She picked up the doll and put it out of sight. The two women continued to regard me with shock.

At last my mother gathered her thoughts. "What if it had

been a real child? I don't think it would have mattered. She'd have killed a child."

There was silence as the three of us sat there, the power of my outburst still filling the small room.

Nobody ever mentioned my violent attack on Sally again. It was too terrible to even think about. I never saw my beautiful doll after that day. I've no idea where she went. She just disappeared. The other Sally, the little girl inside me, remained. In fact she took over more and more of Daddy's loving us, hurting us. Daddy needed to do this to us. He didn't mean to hurt us. He just had to get the white stuff out of him. He loved me very much.

Looking back on the seven-year-old that I was, I get a new, more sinister version of the story of coaxing my father to take me camping. I now suspect the pressure coming from my parents was unbearable. It was vital I scrub those frying pans and get my father to take me camping. In hindsight I think my mother needed me to seduce him, to keep him home with us. If I didn't do my job he'd leave us and return to England to the other woman.

I was the pawn in a nasty adult game of chess. I can only guess that both of them were pleased with their parental decision to keep a promise made to a child. He had a good excuse for a week of sex with me. She had a week of not having to put up with him while at the same time securing her position as his wife.

I think back to the weeks I was keeping house for him while my mother was with my sister and the new baby in Winnipeg. This was the time when I had just escaped from Bishop Strachan School. My father was driving me crazy by eating with his mouth open. Thinking about it now, mouth-smacking noises resemble the sounds of sex. Certainly, the disgust and rage I experienced match the emotions of having been used as a sexual object. But I have no actual memories of incest during this period.

Such is the maddening quality of traumatic memories. They're not like my ordinary memories where, if I try really hard, I can probably recall everyone who came to my birthday party.

My brain needed to assure my survival. Anything I couldn't endure, my child's brain rendered inaccessible, or made available only in fragments. This dissociation helped me to experience many healthy parts of childhood, adolescence, and adulthood. The question remains for me: If I had known I was my family's little courtesan could I have passed through these developmental stages? I have to hand it to myself. For a girl who was often a walking zombie, I did very well at experiencing many of life's normal joys.

I think something else helped me survive my early childhood: a part of myself that never did get wounded. I came across this part during a Focusing session with Mary McGuire in Chicago. During that period I wrote in my journal:

> I've been so tense ever since coming here. Being on the panel [of the International Focusing Conference] brought out a very insecure part of me. It feels like a neglected baby part, the baby my parents didn't want. My own internalized parents' attitude is very unloving. Yet the baby knows it is wonderful! Its sadness comes from the fact that its parents don't think it's adorable. My right side becomes the place where the baby lives. As I say this and am with it, the baby grows and fills out that side. But it's cut off from "me."
>
> The right side of my body seems to be the side that took the abuse. It doesn't trust me to look after it or hold it. It's been abandoned too often. There's a standoff. The

baby barely breathes. I don't feel moved, somehow, to go forward and grab it.

Mary suggests I pretend to hold my own son as a baby. I do and that feels wonderful. The inner baby watches with interest. He begins to have more trust in me. At one point, he pops up to join the cuddling. There needs to be some way of daily holding this cut-off tough little guy. He feels a lot of pride in his ability to survive alone and in his toughness.

A few days later I recorded this:

Tough Little Guy is feeling better about himself and I'm feeling so much tenderness for him. He's stomping about in a diaper and top hat like the New Year's baby, telling me how he doesn't need anybody.

When I returned to Toronto I went to see my psychotherapist, Helen, about this newly discovered part of myself.

Working with her it became evident that the Tough Little Guy is a part of me that was *never* violated. It hid in my right side and let everything happen to the rest of my body, but it *never* got sucked into believing that adults and the world meant well. Its strength is in the feeling "I don't need anybody."

If something terrible happened there *was* nobody to help it and that was the *truth* and the *reality*. It is a sane part of me. It is the *me-ness*.

Chapter 15

You Tell, You Die

"Most children don't tell. Most adults don't tell. It's usually because of overwhelming shame. It's not until mid-life that most people disclose. Many survivors carry their secrets for decades." (Marilyn Van Derbur, Miss America by Day, *p. 461)*

I remember the first time I told my mother about being sexually assaulted. I was seven.

This wasn't about my father or grandfather. I couldn't have told her about them, since at that time, I didn't know myself. One summer following the war we went to a resort in the Laurentians where the popular recreation director kept the children busy. His name was Bert and he liked to carry children high on his shoulders. When it came my turn for the honour of riding on Bert's shoulders I was confused and uncomfortable to realize his hand was inside my underpants rubbing my genitals.

I didn't like it. I also felt ashamed. Troubled, I confided in my sister about what had happened. She assured me he did that to all the children and he'd tried to do the same thing to her. Stay away from him, she advised me. And I did.

What bewildered me most was how much my parents liked Bert. They couldn't understand what he was doing in a small resort when he had the education to get a much better job. Naturally it never occurred to them that he'd found a pedophile's dream job.

It was months later that I decided to tell my mother the truth about Bert. His assault still bothered me and I hoped that, in telling her, I would feel better. No sooner had I got the words out of my mouth than she turned on me.

"You nasty little girl," she almost screamed. "You must have enjoyed it!"

"No," I protested. "I didn't like it."

"Well, if you hadn't enjoyed it, you'd have told me."

It was no use. I'd told her and now she looked on me as a bad girl.

When I was in my forties and my father had been dead for many years I was ready to tell my sister and my mother I had been sexually abused. I knew this was risky. After all I would be telling my sister her father and her grandfather were pedophiles. For my mother, my news would bring dishonour to the family, labelling her husband as a sexual predator and herself as the mother who had not kept me safe. It would be incredibly painful for me if my mother and my sister rejected me and my past, but I longed for their comfort. I wanted them to express sadness for all I had suffered. I wanted them to care about what had happened to me. As well, my father had threatened me with death if I told, and I needed to prove to myself that telling would not be the end of me.

When I first recalled my memories of child sexual abuse I had turned to Helen, my therapist in past years. I needed a professional again to guide me in this new stage of my struggles. Helen cautioned me that she had no training in the area of sexual abuse. But she knew my background and I was an expert in sexual abuse. Together we'd be able to help me. Furthermore, in the eighties there weren't that many psychotherapists trained to treat child sexual abuse.

Two things kept the therapy from being successful. First Helen didn't really believe sexual abuse happened, at least not to anyone she knew. That disbelief was always present in the therapy room, keeping me from truly listening to myself. Then, when I decided I needed to disclose my truth to my mother, Helen, who was elderly herself, identified with my mother. She could not support me in disturbing this aged woman with my painful version of the family.

By this time Dr. Ralph Bierman had arrived in Toronto to set up private practice after a career of teaching experiential psychotherapy in various Canadian universities. We met over lunch a number of times. Realizing he had skills in client-centered therapy that I wanted to learn, I hired him to do some training with my students at The Centre for Focusing. I became aware that this gentle man was alive and joyful in places where I felt deadened. His pleasure in life was palpable. As I got to know him better and was feeling blocked in my work with Helen, I asked him, "Do you think you could help me bring to life the parts of me that feel dead?"

He laughed and assured me it was probably workable. And so I started my regular sessions with him.

He told me he thought I was courageous and that he held me in high regard. Mostly he made a safe space for me to get on with the business of being open to receive the lost memories that were surfacing in my body/mind. He helped me turn down the volume on the inner voices in my head that didn't want me to know what had happened to me.

With Ralph's support I finally decided to tell my sister about my childhood sexual abuse. I asked her to meet me for lunch. Over our meal we exchanged our usual pleasantries as well as the latest news of our mates and our children. My heart was beating loudly as I prepared to open Pandora's box.

With lunch over we moved to an outdoor bench in a private corner of a park near my office building. Here we sat, hidden from view by low bushes. I told her I had something to tell her that was difficult to talk about. She looked at me with a mixture of love and fear. Later she told me she'd been afraid I was going to tell her I had cancer. She was so relieved to hear it was about our father and grandfather that she made it very easy for me. My shocking disclosure couldn't have been better received. No bolt of lightning crashed down from the sky. My sister didn't jump up and tell me I was crazy. Instead we both sat sombrely while she absorbed the story and lovingly stroked my back and shoulder. Her eyes were filled with tears as she remembered "that dear little blonde girl."

She had no trouble believing what I told her about our father, but she simply could not believe her proper old grandfather would act in such a way. She let that remain a mystery and went on to tell me about herself and our father.

She told me how he'd often been inappropriately sexual with her, usually when he was drunk. Mostly she recalled incidents from when she was a teenager or a young, beautiful woman, when he'd leer drunkenly at her, asking if she'd ever made love to a big Swede. The Big Swede was an imaginary character he liked to play when he was drunk. The Big Swede never actually touched her, she said. He was too drunk and she was old enough to handle the situation.

My sister maintained she was certain she'd never been sexually abused. Perhaps our father never assaulted her because she was a twelve-year-old when he returned after a seven-year absence during the war. It's also possible he didn't do so when she was very young since—I believe—he and my mother were happy together during the first years of her life. According to my mother and to the photos in the family album my father was an attentive husband and adored his little daughter.

After the war my sister spent very little time at our house. Instead she practically lived with the older girl next door. I wonder if she was avoiding our father's out-of-control sexual behaviour. That would make sense. My mother attributed her absence to some strange attraction my sister had for the older girl. In retrospect I imagine it was more a matter of revulsion for what lay at home. My sister also escaped by eloping with her boyfriend when she was just sixteen.

My warm feelings about my sister's empathy didn't last long. About a week later she phoned me to say she'd been meditating and had a new understanding of my memories. She said "memories" as if the word smelled bad. She now believed I was suffering burnout from my work with survivors of childhood sexual abuse and I was confusing their memories with my own. That was a perfectly plausible explanation, she went on. It would not be surprising, considering my painful and difficult work. It was no wonder I was suffering vicarious traumatization. Her voice was gentle, her tone caring.

I hung up the phone and dropped into a pit of despair. Once again I had been tossed on the garbage heap by my family. I was furious. I was in agony. I was helpless to make them understand my truth.

I had just found my sister and now she was gone again and I was alone, like that little blonde girl, with my dirty secrets. No one in my family wanted to know what was happening to me, not now and not then.

~~~

Later, when I was finally ready to tell my mother about my abuse, I called to tell her I would come to Stratford for an overnight visit. By this time my son was in high school and I was a practising psychotherapist.

I remember the drive to Stratford. It was a mellow autumn day. The corn stocks stood dried and beige in the fields of Perth County's rolling farmland. The maple groves were crimson and gold, stunning in the light of an October sun.

Why was I doing this? I kept asking myself. Why was I telling her what I'd kept secret for forty years? What was I hoping for from an aged mother whose approval I had finally secured thanks to being the wife of a doctor and her grandson's mother? I wanted to feel better—that's why I was coming to tell her. I wanted to exorcise the memory of my father's fingers on my throat. He had told me I would die if I told her. I needed to prove he was wrong, that I would not die if I told. I wanted her to say she was sorry I had suffered and sorry my life had been made so difficult. I needed her to tell me she was devastated—that she had not been aware and therefore had not protected me. I longed for her to throw her arms around me and tell me how she wished she'd been more alert to the pain and abandonment I'd felt.

I arrived at the house where my mother now rented the upper floor. It was a stately red-brick home the porch of which curved from the front of the house around to the side. Two huge, white wooden horseshoes appeared to hold up the porch's roof. I climbed the stairs to the second floor, knocked on her door, and entered her tastefully decorated apartment with its elaborate plaster cornices and high ceilings. I was anxious and depressed, apprehensive about the outcome of my talk with my mother. To my relief my great-niece was there to provide distraction, at least for a while. I was both eager to get it over with and afraid to set in motion the drama that would follow.

Before dinner, when my mother and I were alone, I announced to her that I needed to talk to her about something. She motioned me to the large green armchair that had been my father's. On previous visits she had voiced her pleasure at having one of her family sit in that amply cushioned chair.

My numbed body dropped stiffly into its soft cushions. It felt like a lap. I stiffened, not allowing the chair to enfold me with its seductive softness.

We sat facing each other, my mother relaxing into her small brocade chair, I bolted upright in the massive armchair. We were surrounded by her ornate bow-front cabinets and paintings by Canadian artists hanging on the walls, her Royal Doulton figurines positioned on small tables around the room: the Balloon Lady, the Sugar Plum Fairy, the yellow ballerina called Tuesday's Child, and purple-gowned Anne Boleyn with her pointed wimple, one of Henry the Eighth's unfortunate wives. I'd grown up with all of them, and now they seemed to be looking at me, filled with reproach.

I could feel my head fuzzing over. Would I be able to speak? The fog was thick inside my skull and I feared passing out. Then I was surprised by an attack from my own inner thoughts. From somewhere inside, something was telling me I'd made it all up. Nothing had happened. I was wrong. I felt like a small, terrified child facing the grownup world's fury at being caught lying. I was making up a terrible lie. I struggled to stay on course and forced myself to begin the conversation I dreaded—and needed.

I began to push the words out of my mouth. My script was carefully rehearsed and shot from my mouth like peas from a pea shooter.

"Mom," I heard my own voice say somewhere in the distance, "I have to tell you something that happened to me a long time ago."

All of my senses were floating in a sea of fog, disconnected from me—and yet I was acutely aware at the same time of how she was receiving me. My heightened senses picked up on how she relaxed on hearing it was a long time ago. Maybe, like my sister, she'd worried I had cancer.

I started in about Grandpa. My mother listened, occasionally breaking into my monologue with, "No! Oh, Mary, darling" and "How terrible!" She was pushing her small body into the brocade chair and, at the same time, pulling herself up to her full height. Her eyes flashed with the fury of a mother whose offspring had been assaulted.

"He had no right to do that!" she spat. "He should have found a woman for sex."

Her rage was clean and clear.

There was no doubt in her mind that he had betrayed her trust when she left him in charge of me while she ran the family business during the war years.

Warming to the subject, she revealed to me how Grandpa had constantly pawed her young body, especially when she was pregnant with my sister. His eyes were lustful and deeply embarrassing. She could not mention it to my father. Nor could she tell my father that on Sundays, when they invited his father and brother for midday dinner, his brother spent the hour after dinner chasing her around the house insisting she wanted to go to bed with him, not with her husband. Meanwhile, my father and grandfather napped after the meal, unaware of what was happening.

The disclosure had gone better than I could have hoped. I decided to try telling her the rest of my story.

"Dad sexually assaulted me, too," I blurted out.

Her face hardened and her eyes narrowed.

In an instant I went from being the wronged child to being the enemy.

I had to be mistaken, she told me. By now I was swimming in a sea of confusion, but I knew I had to hang on to my line of thought. I stuck to my story. She listened to me until the end of my disclosure.

There was a long silence as she struggled to find an explanation. At last she told me that my father often "let go" in the wrong places and at the wrong times. This made me angry.

Realizing she was describing premature ejaculation I couldn't resist firing back. "You mean he couldn't control his penis," I said.

We both fell silent again. Finally I said, "Mom, that's not what I need to talk to you about today. What I need to tell you is that, all during my childhood, my grandfather and my father used me as a sexual outlet."

"Your father only wanted sex when he was drunk," she said. Her gaze was distant, off in some other time and place.

I squirmed, not really wanting to hear about my mother's sex life. I needed her to hear about *my* premature introduction to sex, the assaults that had traumatized *me*.

"As a result of the interference"—I purposely chose a word used by her generation— "there were years and years when I had a hard time having a normal sex life with Harvey."

I could see her brain going to work. Harvey. Yes, this whole unpleasant conversation had to do with Harvey. I wasn't sure where we were in the discussion. My mother looked lost. I was exhausted and anxious at the same time. We agreed to eat dinner in front of the television.

Throughout my youth my mother often told us about a disturbing, recurrent nightmare. It was always the same. She, her mother, my sister, and I were in a pastoral, grassy setting in the sunshine. The children were gambolling like lambs in the long grass. Suddenly there was a sinister change. Something was terribly wrong. The sky darkened and the long grass was wet and slimy. My mother was repulsed and horrified. She couldn't stand the feeling of the wet grass on her legs. She tried to find her children, who were in great danger. She always wakened in a cold sweat from this nightmare.

I think she always knew at some level about the abuse. She spent a lot of time convalescing in bed. Although she lived almost to the age of ninety-four, she was never really robust and viewed herself as bravely dealing with chronic ill health.

The morning after I had summoned up my courage to tell her about my childhood incest, she complained to me that her sleep had been disturbed by my story and she hoped I felt better for having upset her this way. She didn't seem to comprehend the pain that incest had caused me, leaving me with years of nightmares and disturbed sleep, among so many other problems.

I looked at her and struggled for something to say, something that would demonstrate the insignificance of a troubled night compared with a troubled lifetime. No words came. Maybe now that she knew, she would begin to feel my pain. She was really lucky to have reached her advanced age without being burdened by our family's dirty secret. I was the one who bore the pain. At last, having no adequate words, I simply said goodbye and headed for my car.

Appearances were always of paramount importance to my mother. In the months to follow, rather than revise her version of her perfect family she preferred to view me as disturbed and delusional. This was how she handled the unacceptable news

I had brought her. Her rationale served her well. She didn't have to ask herself why she hadn't managed to protect me. She could pity her emotionally unbalanced daughter. I could see her deciding that Harvey was putting ideas into my vulnerable mind. I was too easily influenced. In short she avoided searching her soul for corroboration or being open to the possibility that I had indeed been sexually abused by the males in our household. She refused to acknowledge my suffering.

Christmas came a couple of months after I had told her about my childhood sexual abuse. She came to stay at our house for the holiday. She and I had never mentioned my disclosure since my initial talk with her. I expected we would revisit the subject during her visit.

I was in the kitchen when Harvey joined my mother for a drink in the living room. He sat down beside her, took her hand in his, and told her I had been feeling a lot better since my memories surfaced and I realized what I had been struggling with all these years. She pulled her hand back and barked, "Nothing happened back there and if it had I'd have stopped it like that." She snapped her fingers.

I felt the sting of her reaction. We never mentioned it again. Thus began many years of polite, perfunctory interactions.

She had not paid attention when I was a child. She had chatted away for many years before I knew why her bright chatter made me angry. And now that she knew my pain she continued to chatter away, oblivious to my discomfort. I had told her what had happened and she still chose not to know that bad things had happened to me.

The abandonment of my mother and sister was both hurtful and familiar. It would always remain as it had been in childhood. My sister would dismiss my pain. My mother's narcissistic chatter would continue, and she'd be oblivious to the awful things that had happened right under her nose. Once more my mother was choosing herself instead of me. She'd refused to recognize what was happening when I was a helpless child. She was choosing to deny my pain again.

Many years after first telling my sister I tried again to expose my wounded self to her. It was Christmastime. When I called her on the telephone she asked how I was and instead of the usual reply of "Just fine, thanks," I decided to be truthful. I told her the Christmas season was always difficult for me because, as I recalled, our father always managed to get home from overseas during the war when we were children. My memories of him are very frightening, I said, but didn't go into details. I could hear her trying to be kind and compassionate on the other end of the line, but this was evidently leaving her speechless. There was a long pause.

"Really?" she finally said.

What did she mean?

"Don't you remember this about me and him?" I asked her.

"No."

She didn't remember our earlier conversations when I'd told her about our father and my childhood sexual abuse.

I didn't go on to remind her about Grandpa. That one had been too hard for her to take in the first time around.

In that conversation and in a subsequent one she seemed to be assuring herself that my memory was faulty. Did I remember the year we had turkey hash for Christmas dinner? Because that was a year Dad didn't get home. You see, he didn't get home every Christmas as I thought. In fact there were a couple of Christmases when he didn't make it home at all ...

Chapter 16

The Wonderful Years

I turned fifty in 1988 and a whole new decade of adventures opened up to me. I'd gone from being a helpless victim to a woman who could have a vision and make it materialize. I was no longer powerless to direct my own life.

In the seven years since graduating from the School of Social Work I'd successfully established a private practice as a social work psychotherapist; this despite the fact that my fees were not covered by government insurance or extended health coverage. When people have to pay they don't come back unless you really are helping them.

But that wasn't all. This was the time when Gendlin (who was still a professor of psychology at the University of Chicago) suggested I open a Focusing centre in Toronto to connect with the Focusing Institute he planned to establish in Chicago. It was an exciting dream and fit with my purpose in life, which was—and still is—to connect myself and others with our own deepest, wisest selves.

When Harvey started talking about going into private practice it made practical sense for us to rent space together. By then I'd been in practice long enough to risk a change. Between 1980, when I first opened my practice, and 1987, when we were thinking of joining forces, I had gained confidence in my skills as a therapist. I still felt somewhat anxious about being overshadowed by Harvey. After all he had twenty years of experience and was well recognized in the community. I didn't want to be known as "Armstrong's wife."

In the end we decided to rent a suite of offices large enough for the organization he named Parents for Youth and for my Centre for Focusing. Thus began our two decades of working side by side at Yonge Street and St. Clair Avenue. Our offices on the ninth floor, with their huge windows overlooking the city, were inviting and comfortable.

As it turned out we did very well. We supported each other, passing each other in the hall on days when we were both too busy to stop for meals together. It was the beginning of a period in both our lives when we were totally committed to our professional work. We threw ourselves into our callings with a passion. We both had a mission. We shared an urgency to help those who had been injured by childhood trauma. We learned everything we could about physical, emotional, and, especially, sexual abuse.

Knowledge of psychological trauma was in its infancy during this time. In Canada very little was understood by mainstream professionals. Treatment of traumatized people was left to grassroots helpers. We had to travel to the U.S. to learn from experienced practitioners who had practical knowledge of dissociation and the invisible wounds we were encountering in our clients and patients. Usually we went to Chicago to attend the meetings of the International Society for the Study of Multiple Personality and Dissociation (ISSMPD). There we learned from teachers who actually had years of experience in treating the signs and symptoms of child abuse we were helping clients with back home in our offices. The ISSMPD still exists under the name International Society for the Study of Trauma and Dissociation (ISSTD), but the diagnosis "multiple personality disorder" is no longer used. "Dissociative identity disorder" is the current name, reflecting the disorder's place at the extreme end of the dissociative scale.

Chicago was drawing me for another reason. The Focusing Institute found a home in the Fine Arts Building on Michigan Avenue. I remember the thrill of arriving at O'Hare Airport for my frequent visits to learn still more about this new life that was opening up for me. To this day any time I arrive at that airport and ride along the moving sidewalks with the beautifully coloured neon tubes swimming above me, my heart soars.

Back home I started teaching Focusing in my office on Monday evenings, after I'd finished with clients. At first I designed a course that followed the six steps of Focusing. Gendlin's six-step model, as described in *Focusing*, is easy to teach and, if students are ready, it can take them to some very deep places. The advantage of such a structured course was that students could follow what they were learning from me in Gendlin's paperback. It gave them something concrete on which to build a new skill.

In time some students were ready to learn more than the basic skills of Focusing. At this point I organized a second level of teaching. Beginners met at 5:30. More advanced students came at 7:30. Students settled into a comfortable circle of couches and chairs. The huge windows in the room opened up to the wide sky with its scudding clouds, brilliant sunsets, the moon and stars, or the wind and rain. The setting inspired a sense of safety and creativity.

Second-level courses were all ten weeks long with titles like Focusing and Health, Focusing and Couples, Focusing and Trauma, and Focusing and the Critic.

The Institute started certifying serious students as Focusing trainers. These people were recognized as competent to teach others to Focus and to accompany others in Focusing. Gendlin had a vision of a world in which everyone would know how to Focus. All individuals would set aside time each day to access their own inner lives. Also, all Focusers would have at least one Focusing partner, a peer relationship in which equals sat down and listened to one another or kept each other company in the Focusing process.

When an issue didn't resolve itself with a Focusing partner the person would go to a Focusing trainer, a person skilled in Focusing who probably got paid. If the trainer couldn't help, then the one with the problem would go to a professional. This meant that the professional had to offer skills and knowledge the others lacked, because highly effective professionals charge healthy fees.

Through Focusing I learned to pay attention to how my body responded to absolutely anything. I could ask my body and it would provide me with physically felt answers—like that first weekend workshop with the two priests when I'd asked my body how it felt about Focusing and my whole torso expanded with the most wonderful openness. The image of a balloon emerged. I was holding the balloon by a string. The balloon lifted me up and I flew through the sky, looking down on the earth below. I could see it all. I knew I had found the answer to my future path. This was the overview I needed.

I was training a handful of special people in Toronto to join me in the venture of developing Focusing in the city. We met for a weekend retreat. I needed to gain a clear vision of a management strategy. I asked my body how it felt about opening a Focusing centre. Again there was a balloon. Only this time it was a big hot-air balloon. I was in the basket steering it with the ropes, watching the burner's flames fill my purple balloon.

I looked around my basket and suddenly felt very lonely. Where were all the others who had joined me in this venture? I was all alone in the basket. Filled with disappointment I looked out at the sky. And then I saw it! All around, flying independently, were other balloons. And in each balloon was one of the people I valued enough to train. There was Glenith! There was Danita! There was Kevin! There was Mary B.! There was Kay! And there was Catherine! Each of them dear to my heart. The remarkable thing was that each of them was in a different-coloured balloon. They were all pulling their own strings, flying their own balloons.

That knowing established the management strategy and the philosophy that would become the Centre for Focusing. I would train students to be teachers and then it was up to them to filter the teaching through their own strengths and interests.

Choosing students who were to become Focusing trainers (teachers), to be certified by Gendlin's Focusing Institute, demanded careful thought on my part. Focusing needs client-centred attention where the teacher is deeply committed to believing the answers and the wisdom lie within the student. Somebody interested in having power over another or in appearing smart would misuse the gift of Focusing. I also wanted to be sure my students would not hang up their shingles as therapists on the basis of my courses. There is a big difference between a Focusing trainer, who is qualified to teach Focusing and accompany someone in Focusing, and a Focusing therapist or Focusing-Oriented psychotherapist with years of training, the right background for their special field, and supervised practice.

Early training took place on the weekends, usually out in the country. I would teach some aspect of facilitating Focusing. Then the students would practise this in pairs. The training was intense and personal.

Every time I had a problem, needed a perspective from my wiser self, or just wanted to calm down, I Focused. It became my touchstone for knowing. I no longer needed another strong person to tell me what to think. I had my own way of tapping into a source of knowing. This source of knowing was uncontaminated by anyone else, drawing from my deepest, wisest self a truth that was all my own.

I was learning to follow my dharma, to be "a co-creator with God," as Swami Radha had urged. In practical terms this meant that if something wasn't working out, I was prepared to drop it, understanding the block as a message that this wasn't the right way to go. Following one's dharma is tricky and subtle. It does not mean giving up easily or being lazy. It means not wasting your energy going in directions you're not meant to follow.

During the years I founded and directed the Centre for Focusing I worked very hard. In fact I lived, ate, and slept Focusing and the Centre. My mission was to train as many people as possible. Imagine how wonderful the world would be if everyone had a Focusing partner to simply listen empathically—if people knew how to access their own wisest knowing and we all respected one another's differences, rather than trying to overpower each other.

Eugene Gendlin came to our first Toronto graduation of Focusing trainers, and presented the certificates to the graduates. We cleared the large waiting/reception area in the suite of offices I shared with Harvey for a weekend workshop with

Gene. Sitting on couches, chairs, and cushions on the floor, a couple of dozen Focusing students learned from the master in what was a remarkable gathering of psychotherapists, body workers, art therapists, teachers, nurses, and anybody else who aspired to live more fully and consciously.

During this time I organized and ran a couple of retreats each year. From Friday evening to late Sunday afternoon a couple of dozen Focusers would settle into a weekend of teaching, small group work, and fun. The settings were definitely conducive to enjoyment and comfort. I learned from Swami Radha that people needed to feel comfortable to learn. If they were distracted by lumpy beds, food they weren't accustomed to, or a sense of being unsafe, their energy would be spent in trying to adjust, rather than in immersing themselves in learning.

One of our retreat settings was in the Hockley Valley, an easy drive from Toronto. We settled into an old farmhouse and a renovated barn with many bedrooms, each with its own distinctive, colourful quilt. The barn's orange-carpeted meeting room was originally built as a yoga room. It was perfect for our purposes. Outside, walking trails wound through the hills and valleys, inviting participants to walk and reflect or simply sit under a tree on one of the many logs or benches provided for that purpose. Caring, well-taught trainers made for a sense of safety. It was a time of rich personal growth for all of us, both participants and leaders.

Another setting was the old Roman Catholic convent school overlooking Niagara Falls. Here again the rooms were comfortable and the setting offered beauty, a stress-free environment, and a most amazing view of the falls. We always went there in October when there were few tourists and we could pretty much have the falls to ourselves. Over and over I witnessed the power of this amazing setting to enlarge and enrich each participant's sense of self. Each one seemed to take from the grandeur of the falls whatever energy he or she needed to move forward in life.

Eugene Gendlin was excited by the spirit of our retreat and full of praise for the Centre's Focusing attitude in action, where compassionate, skilled trainers created an environment of safety and openness for participants.

The Focusing Institute was spreading its wings, too. Now there were yearly international conferences. The first of them were held in Chicago. This was where I got to know Focusers from around the world, many of whom became valued friends. Each year I presented my work—what I was doing and what my new edge was. My presentations were received with enthusiasm and praise. I was being recognized as a person with much to offer to the world of Focusing.

Soon I was receiving invitations to teach in Europe. For a decade I travelled to Germany twice a year, teaching Focusing students, psychotherapy students, and psychotherapists. I took to them whatever augmented their own excellent program.

In Weingarten, a small and ancient town in the Black Forest, two colleagues—Heijo Feuerstsein and Dieter Müller—ran Focusing Zentrum Karlsruhe.

My first visit with them was unforgettable. I arrived via the Netherlands where I had been teaching, to be met at the Frankfurt airport by Heijo. We drove to Dieter's home, which was attached to the Focusing Zentrum Karlsruhe, for a meal with his family. Once the weekend sessions began on Friday evening we came back to Dieter's house, to the Focusing centre, which was located behind his house. A courtyard separated the modern centre from Dieter's traditional house. We walked through a gate, past the students' bicycles to the second floor of a building that housed the airy, open space of the classroom. The students greeted one another and welcomed me.

I felt as if I was with my own students in Toronto, except these students were speaking German. However, for these patient people it didn't seem to be much of a problem that I didn't speak German. From the first workshop I developed what I called "International Speak": slow, carefully enunciated English with the agreement that as soon as anyone missed what I was saying, he or she would let me know and someone would translate it into German. It worked very well. Of course they all spoke and understood English, even if some were a bit rusty.

In the nineties I began teaching them about post-traumatic stress disorder. I was learning that Germany had a well-documented history of "black pedagogy"—officially sanctioned traumatic child-rearing. Add this to the country's historical and more recent war trauma and Germany had to be the Western world's most traumatized nation. Yet it had no real body of literature on trauma. Any available books were in English. (The last time I was in Germany, at a conference in Berlin, I noted tables of books for sale on PTSD, trauma, child sexual abuse, and all of the subject areas that needed to be available, all in German.)

This was a rich and wonderful ten-year chapter in my life. The students were as responsive and as open to my teaching as my own students back home. Over time my German colleagues became good friends. I came to know their children and their parents.

A psychotherapist has a privileged window on the lives of individuals and on society. I treasure my understanding of this country with its troubled history.

As the years passed Gendlin's Focusing Institute became more international, and international conferences were held only once every four years in the U.S. Yearly I travelled to a different country—the U.S., Ireland, Costa Rica, the Netherlands, Germany, and so on—presenting my work and learning from other Focusers.

The reality of my life was far surpassing any hopes I may have had for myself.

In 2000 my own centre hosted the annual International Focusing Conference. Focusers from around the world gathered north of Toronto for four days of workshops, small group work, and the exchange of ideas.

Our planning began two years before the conference. There were nine of us on the team responsible for carrying out this daunting task. My role was to support the team and run our meetings. As we drew closer to the date of the conference tempers naturally frayed. Team members, including me, grew anxious about the outcome. By now we were meeting at least twice a week in my office.

As chair of our meetings I asked each person to hold off discussing their issues until we sat down for some quiet time together. Then I led them through a relaxation exercise, asking each person to breathe slowly and to notice what was happening inside of them. I reminded them that we all wished to come from the quiet, calm place inside of us. We needed to bring our "big selves" to the task at hand.

It worked, and I figured if we planned the whole conference in this caring spirit, the same atmosphere would naturally carry us into the four days of the conference.

Our job was to look after the participants arriving from the different countries. If we were to do a good job looking after *them*, somebody had to look after us.

At the conference site I set aside a special room just for our team. It was a place where we met to support one another at the beginning and end of each day, and any time an issue arose for someone. I spent a lot of time in that room, making myself available to team members. It was a great experience for everyone, team members and participants. For me it was a small example of how organizations and businesses could be run. The world of commerce would be so different if it were structured to care for the individuals who serve it.

Almost thirty years after the start of my professional life I look back with a sense of gratitude and fullness at all life gave me the chance to do: developing a centre where people found belonging and enriched their lives with new insights and deeper empathy; being a psychotherapist to people with the courage to look inside and heal their wounds; and travelling and teaching in other countries where I learned so much from the students and the foreign lands.

And what about my mother during the Wonderful Years? While I was beginning to age myself, my mother was doing remarkably well for a woman in her late eighties and early nineties. I appreciated her as a role model of how to enjoy life as an elderly person. She was still lively and involved in life. In my journal around that time I wrote: "This morning when I looked in the mirror, it was my mother's knowing eyes looking back at me. I warmed with love at the sight of her. This is the mother I love. It's as if there are two mothers—the one who didn't protect me and the one I love."

My feelings for her were so confused. If I'd met her for the first time when I was an adult, I'd have seen her differently. I'm sure I would have warmed to her and found her likeable.

Since I consider myself a loving person the hate I sometimes felt for her was embarrassing and bewildering. Being an expert in child abuse I know this is a normal way to feel about the non-abusing parent who fails to protect the child. All the intensity of my rage was directed towards her, perhaps because I viewed her as powerful enough to have saved me.

My father got off easy. Strangely, I could never work up a real head of rage for him, the perpetrator. Instead I look on him as pathetic and spineless, unable to control his self-indulgent perversion.

Chapter 17

Life as a Trauma Therapist

People—especially my clients—frequently ask how I can spend so much of my life listening to others' problems. This always surprises me, because I consider my job the most fascinating and rewarding work on earth. Actually I don't even think of it as a job. It is a calling, and it is certainly not depressing.

If you decide to work with me and tell me about the problems for which you want my help, I listen for ways in which you and I can change how you carry your issues. The troublesome people in your life are unlikely to change and we can seldom alter the external world.

What we can transform is our inner world—the way in which we respond emotionally to a situation. We can make healthier decisions for ourselves, maybe deciding to get out of a job or relationship. We can do the necessary trauma treatment so our adult emotions, not those of our hurt inner child, are determining our reactions.

I have many, many ways of helping people make whatever changes are uniquely right for them. Only the client, a unique organism in the universe, knows what is right for him or her. I seldom give advice. I do teach clients to access their own deepest, wisest knowing.

When you phone to book a first appointment I am aware it took courage for you to take this step. You are risking exposing your vulnerability in the hope of receiving help. Maybe the therapist will treat your frailty with disrespect. Maybe you've been "mounted" by arrogant professionals in the past, given the message that you're weak and not very smart while the therapist remains the one who is clever and wise. Worse, maybe a previous therapist has told you what you're *really* thinking. Possibly you're anxious about changing. After all it's scary to enter therapy knowing you're willingly subjecting yourself to becoming someone different. That means dropping your old ways of coping, giving up thoughts and behaviours you once believed kept you out of harm's way. Maybe you want to be more relaxed. But that means letting go of the hyper-vigilance that deep down you've always believed keeps you safe.

Before anything much can happen in therapy, you have to feel safe with the therapist. Connecting with one's own deepest, wisest places requires this. Most clients seem relieved on the first meeting that I look normal and competent. We humans heal in relationships, so right away you and I will begin to establish a therapeutic relationship.

What is a therapeutic relationship? It is a relationship that exists for the sole purpose of taking care of the client's needs. The therapist asks only that you come and leave on time, pay your bill, and do your work. In this way it is different from usual reciprocal relationships. It is not a friendship, although you and I may come to care deeply for each other. It is my job to learn, as much as is humanly possible, what it's like to be you. To this end I listen with a concentration reserved for therapy. I don't need to be conscious of my body language, the correct way to sit, and so on. If I am truly present, my facial expression and body posture will reflect that. I will, however, be very aware of *your* body language. Everyone is uniquely fascinating once you get to know them. I will find out all about you, but disclose my own thoughts and experiences only when I deem it valuable to your healing.

In recent years there has been concern over physical touching in therapy. Is a hug okay? Is it acceptable to hold a frightened client's hand or put an arm around a troubled client? Many therapists have been scared off from comforting clients because of charges of sexual harassment against physicians, mental health professionals, teachers, and others in positions of trust.

A serious problem does exist where those with power over others use their positions of trust to sexually abuse the very people who look to them for guidance. But rather than deal with this problem rationally, society responds with hysterical, overblown warnings to professionals about not touching those with whom they work. Teachers cannot put an arm around a child. The therapist is advised not to hold a troubled client's hand.

This, to me, is ridiculous. Everyone knows the difference between sexual touch and comforting touch. It's time we recognized the prevalence of sexual predators in our society. By denying their presence we end up fearing we could be accused of sexual improprieties. Except for the odd, inevitable miscarriage of justice, the accused are generally guilty as charged.

I like to be face to face with clients. Usually we sit facing each other in two chairs. You and I will take a moment to determine a comfortable distance between us—not so close that I'm encroaching on your personal space and not so far that we become disconnected. Right away we are establishing respect for our personal boundaries. We are not about to become one entity. There is an I-Thou in therapy. I will try as much as is humanly possible to empathize with your experience of life. But I am a separate being, having my own experience of you. I use this personal experience to better understand what's going on for you. In the jargon of psychotherapy, this is my counter-transference. (Your experience of me is your transference.)

As I listen to you I invite you to drop into your body, into your own internal life. I will try very hard not to distract you from that connection with yourself. This is where your wisdom lies. It is my job to help you go deeper without getting in your way.

For example, if I say something and your eyebrows lift, I know my words have taken you into your head. I've made a mistake and will quickly try to get us back on track by saying something like, "Just let that go. You were saying ..."

I am your companion on your journey, carrying one end of your awkward two-by-four. A two-by-four is very hard to carry alone, but easy with someone on the other end. I stay with you and never get ahead of you. I may think I know where you are going but I never lead the way. That could be disempowering— and disconcerting—for you. Finding your own path is central to your journey of healing.

As the therapist I am always looking for that place where you are alive and have good energy. We need to bring this good energy along with us to balance out the pain of the issues you bring to therapy. If you are depressed I may ask, "Is there anything in your life which is not totally bleak?" When you tell me about your beloved dog or grandchild or the taste of your favourite ice cream, I will encourage you to stay with and appreciate that pleasure. We'll likely add one pleasure on top of the other until the heavy, gray place inside is filled with good feeling.

I will spend time educating you about your emotional state. It's important for you to know I understand your situation. And it's also important that you understand what is happening to make you feel so bad. I am your strong ally, lending you my strength and clarity. Even if you're dealing with something painful and difficult, you will almost always leave my office feeling better. You may have discovered something upsetting, but you will feel a sense of hope.

In the process of Focusing-Oriented Psychotherapy you will come to realize that something is alive inside you. You have a rich inner life! Maybe you never realized this before. I encourage you to stay with the uncomfortable body sensations that are about your life. This may be the tightness in your chest or the lump in your throat. My psychological mentor, Dr. Eugene Gendlin, describes it this way in his book *Focusing*:

> Every bad feeling is potential energy toward a more right way of being if you give it space to move toward its rightness.
>
> The very existence of bad feelings within you is evidence that your body knows what is wrong and what is right. It must know what it would be like to feel perfect, or it could not evoke a sense of wrong. (p. 76)

The body holds our problems like a cramp. When you are with the uncomfortable feeling in a caring, compassionate way, the cramp releases and you gain access to the previously unconscious knowing.

Focusing is safe. It's gentle, like the proverbial drip on the rock. You won't suddenly be faced with something you're not ready to look at.

But resistance may rise up to block new knowing. Your mind may wander or your head may fill with fog. You may suddenly feel very sleepy. We view resistance, whatever its form, as protection. We establish a relationship with the resistance. After all it's there because at one time it was protecting you. We need to cooperate with it, and when we do, resistance gradually gives way. Working in this way you will come to know your own life story safely—and uncontaminated by a therapist's advice or views on life.

Most of the above I learned from Dr. Gendlin's compassionate, highly effective ways of helping clients heal from the wounds of child abuse and neglect. In March 1991 he held a workshop for Focusing psychotherapists in Chicago's Fine Arts Building. There, in this historic building with its gilded elevator cage and massive, ornate doors, he presented his new theory of the "blueprint." Twenty to thirty of us from around the world sat in a circle in a large, high-ceilinged room. We were there to take in the wisdom of the man who inspired us to view clients, mental illness, and ourselves in a different light.

Gene took his place and settled in to teach us. His body is lanky and he wore a white cotton shirt with the sleeves rolled up and the neck comfortably open. He crossed one brown pants leg over the other and leaned forward to greet each of us in turn. The ever-present cigarette package bulged in his shirt pocket.

The teaching started and he reminded us that as Focusing-Oriented Therapists we all knew that when one keeps a stuck place company, there is a sense of expecting something to come there, for steps to move towards there. We ask that place in us what it needs to get unstuck, to move forward with our lives. As therapists we know this works and the organism knows how to move forward. Even if our life situations have never happened before in the world, the body somehow knows what should happen next. The body comes up with something totally new. The body knows a further step that hasn't yet happened.

Gene tipped his chair back. Spreading his hands over the middle of his body, he looked around the circle. "Are we getting it so far?" he seemed to be asking himself. Evidently he decided we were with him and continued.

He told us he'd known what he'd just taught us for a long time. Today, though, he had something new to teach us. He'd figured out why the body knows the next step, even though it had never experienced that situation before.

The infant, he explained, carries a blueprint of what hasn't happened yet. After birth an infant's body is organized based on what should happen next. If there's a breast waiting with that clear fluid that's somehow just right for the newborn, the baby is happy. If something goes wrong the baby is very unhappy. And so it is throughout our lives.

Gene leaned his head back and clasped his hands behind his neck. So, he told us, when we're dealing with clients we need to say, "It shouldn't have gone that way"; "You should have had the sort of parents you needed"; "Children should be loved and protected"; "I know all that good stuff didn't happen, but it should have."

The part of the client that knows how it should have been was silenced in childhood. And it's that part, the part that knows what should have happened, that is the most life-sourcing part of the person. That part stirs when you say, "That shouldn't have happened."

We took a coffee break so Gene could go out for a smoke. When he returned he looked as if he was trying very hard to get us to take in something difficult. He looked around at each of us again, silently asking, "Are you with me?"

What he wanted us to understand is that what *should* have happened is more real than what actually happened. He told us that what happened was, in a way, an accident. Those people, the parents, were so limited. What *should have* happened is more real to the organism.

In therapy, over a period of time and a number of steps, the organism begins to fill in what should have happened. When a client says she feels terrible about what happened in her childhood she is already recognizing what didn't happen—and this leads to what should have happened. As she's talking about what's missing, it's happening for her. The people in her life whom she describes as good parents are becoming integrated into her. The void starts filling itself in. The therapist's job is to make this more present in any way possible.

During the years of absorbing Gene Gendlin's teaching I had a large measure of success in treating survivors of childhood abuse and neglect. I was discovering many ways of helping clients live more fully in the present. As well as Focusing-Oriented Therapy, I prescribed relaxation, mindfulness, and yoga or some other physical exercise, since all of these practices are helpful in healing. Yet there always seemed to be uncomfortable, lingering experiences. Even after years of treatment my clients (and I) could still be triggered into panic by an innocuous event in the present, a harmless event that pulled us into a past, terrifying situation. It was very hard to put the frightening past into the past. The benign present can feel like the terrifying past when you feel your safety threatened, just like when someone startles you from behind. The resulting emotion destabilizes one's inner life and, worse, can cause feelings of shame for the seemingly irrational reaction.

One May I was at the International Focusing Conference being held in Chicago and a group of women were invited to a colleague's home for a pyjama party. Our host was psychologist Bonnie Holstein. Bonnie's husband and daughters were away, she told us, so there was plenty of room at her house.

We spent the evening talking about—what else?—our work. Bonnie described a new technique she was learning that was bringing startling results to her work with trauma clients. The technique is called Eye Movement, Desensitization, and Reprocessing, or EMDR. She was able to help people with it in a way that had not been available before this new therapy. Bonnie described how she waved her fingers back and forth in front of someone's eyes.

"I know it sounds hokey," she said.

"It certainly does," I agreed.

Francine Shapiro, a psychologist, discovered this approach to the healing of trauma when she herself was experiencing trauma in her life. Shapiro went for a walk and found herself feeling surprisingly better. What had happened? Her eyes, she noted, had been moving from side to side as she walked. This rapid eye movement is the way our eyes move when we are dreaming. Dreaming is the organism's way of handling our day-to-day emotions, our body's attempt to keep us from being overwhelmed by our feelings. Curious, Shapiro began experimenting with some of her colleagues.

I was intrigued. Returning to Toronto I searched for someone trained in EMDR. Psychologist Helen Doan at York University was recommended.

I went to see Helen with some of my own material. I chose to work on my memory of my father choking me at Christmastime after sexually abusing me. Helen waved her fingers back and forth and had me follow them with my eyes while I processed the memory of my father. The results were remarkable. In that session I saw my father coming at me with his hands outstretched, about to choke me. His hands stopped in midair. He couldn't move. Gradually he faded from my view and I felt a sense of enormous relief.

I told Harvey that EMDR was indeed something different from anything we knew. This led to our going to the U.S. for training, because nobody was teaching the method in Canada. For the next year or so we practised on each other and hesitatingly introduced it to clients.

About the time Francine Shapiro was instructing others in EMDR, researchers began talking about the workings of the brain: how there are two hemispheres, the cognitive left and the emotional right, and how the limbic system plays a significant role in trauma.

When the brain has been traumatized the emotional, right side of the brain cannot access the rational thinking of the left brain. Most of us have had an experience with something in our lives that does not make logical sense. We can talk to ourselves about an elevator phobia or a fear of flying but it doesn't change the way we feel. Somehow the two halves of the brain need access to each other. EMDR theory demonstrates that the eye movements allow for bilateral stimulation of the two halves, thus changing the way we experience an event.

The amygdala, part of the brain's limbic system, is central in forming and storing memories associated with emotional events. It is also the emotional watchdog of the limbic system. Any time it senses danger it sends the body into a state of fight or flight. This happens so fast we're not aware it's firing. Before we know it we've jumped out of the path of the oncoming truck. This is adaptive. It saves our lives. Similarly when an adult is afraid of sex with a loving partner, the amygdala is reacting to an old situation and preventing normal behaviour in the present.

I have successfully treated a wide range of cases with EMDR, cases in which reactions don't make rational sense: the fear of rape victims who act as if the perpetrator is still a danger; accident victims who react as if the horrific event is about to reoccur any time they get into a car; an extreme skier who falls off a mountain and keeps restaging the fall on the icy sidewalk outside her home; people who have been in a fire and cannot sleep at night; and, of course, the many men and women who were abused as children and go on living as if the abuse is happening in the present.

Any technique is only that—a technique. To be effective it must be grounded in the experience of the therapist. The therapist using EMDR, for example, must be comfortable with strong emotions and have a thorough understanding of psychological trauma. The therapist needs to provide a sense of safety to the client who is about to uncover what was previously too scary to unveil.

The best approach I know for healing trauma is Focusing. Focusing teaches the client to be compassionate and accepting of any information that bubbles up from previously hidden levels of awareness. It works *around* resistance, which is understood as protection that was needed at one time in the person's life. Taking a battering ram to defences only strengthens them. Focusing teaches an attitude towards one's self of acceptance and of welcoming whatever thoughts or feelings present themselves. In a way the client learns to be her own understanding therapist between sessions and after the therapy is over.

I learn so much, especially from my clients. The children I have worked with have taught me that trauma is cumulative. It is relatively easy to work with a young person's trauma, to change the biochemistry and neurobiology resulting from their trauma. The layers upon layers normally built up in adults following a traumatic event do not exist in a young person. For instance, in my own life, child sexual abuse and my mother's narcissism left me without a self. This led to the further bad experiences and traumatic events described in this book.

The youngest child I have worked with was four years old. This little boy had been sexually abused by his grandfather, a man who had also sexually abused his mother, who brought the little guy to therapy. It was hard for the four-year-old to concentrate for long. We had short sessions and lots of play with finger puppets about whatever was going on in his life (he was being bullied at school). After our EMDR sessions he would sleep soundly for a long time. In fact sleeping soundly is a common outcome of this therapy. His mother reported that after several sessions, he felt much better about himself, was less timid, and was less apt to be bullied.

Another boy, this one a seven-year-old, could not sleep at night, was afraid to go upstairs alone, wet the bed, and kept disturbing his parents' sleep with his frightening nightmares. His mother, a lawyer, sat in a corner of my office while he and I worked. Once the child and I had built a relationship, he told me of the complex system of fierce warriors who waited outside his bedroom window at night. More were under his bed, so he feared getting out of bed to go to the washroom. Terrifying monsters came after him in his dreams.

We never did discover an original trauma. Maybe it was birth trauma. His mother certainly described a difficult labour. Also part of his fears centred on the chimney in their living room where he worried some creature would grab him and pull him up through the fireplace.

Whatever the origin of his awful fears, our EMDR sessions freed him of all these irrational thoughts. As far as I know he has been trauma-free ever since.

Another child I worked with was an eleven-year-old girl. This little girl's life was being ruined by obsessive-compulsive disorder (OCD). She could not climb stairs without ritualistically kicking each step and each riser. Before she could sleep at night she had to go through elaborate routines lasting over an hour. All night she kept waking to check on the time. Needless to say, her peers were avoiding her, finding her weird.

She had been to all the specialists who treated this disabling disease. I knew from my reading that OCD is related to the brain's functioning and EMDR practitioners had been successful in treating it. Since the child had already been treated by the experts I figured there was nothing to lose and agreed to take her on for EMDR therapy. That was in March. By the time school was over at the end of June she was symptom-free. (An adult client of mine no longer suffered the symptoms of severe OCD as a result of her therapy with me. This woman entered therapy not for OCD but to relieve the pain of childhood physical abuse. The OCD healing was almost incidental to the main goal of treatment.)

Carol was a more recent client. She is an extreme skier who fell off a mountain in the Andes. She should have died but, in an act of extraordinary willpower, managed to walk with her husband and guide from the trackless foot of the mountain to their resort for help. You can imagine her chagrin when, a year after the accident, she was shaking, reliving the fall, and restaging her accident by falling backwards (just as she had off the mountain) on the sidewalk in front of her home.

This daring skier sat in my office trembling, unable to control her quivering body. She was embarrassed and impatient with herself. Carol understood, intellectually, that she needed to be compassionate and gentle with her trembling body, but her whole life had been about pushing herself to conquer fear.

Subsequently she wrote the book *Fall Line*, telling of her experience and her healing in therapy with me. EMDR was the treatment that helped her through her trauma, along with the attitudinal gentleness of Focusing. It wasn't long before she reported no disturbing symptoms. Her situation was a single-incident trauma, a temporary disruption in an otherwise fortunate life. Such traumas heal quickly with Focusing and EMDR.

Many of my clients have worked with me for numerous years. These are people whose early lives have left them with multiple traumas and deep wounds from child neglect or child physical, emotional, or sexual abuse. Something in the present usually brings them into therapy: relationship difficulties, a car accident that renders them helpless (feeling like a hurt child), or a life that is finally secure enough to allow memories to surface. The therapeutic relationship with a trustworthy, non-exploitative, respectful person is central to their recovery. Focusing helps them access their own strengths in a compassionate relationship with themselves. EMDR is the surgery, making it possible to correctly store the traumatic past.

The life of a clinician presents constant opportunities for personal growth. In fact I have never stopped growing and learning in my decades as a therapist. The psychotherapist is constantly checking her own emotional response to the client's material. This countertransference contains valuable information for the therapist. Is the anger I'm feeling related to how my client is feeling? Or is my reaction something I need to take care of myself?

Besides the continuous demand to be open to your own inner life, being a psychotherapist requires constantly updating one's training and knowledge. It is a field that is always fresh with new understanding of the human psyche. The more the therapist knows, the better the therapy—provided the therapist sets aside her own theories and knowledge when it's time to become attuned to the client's inner life. There's a place for both, for theoretical knowing and for simply surrendering to the client's experience of life, understanding another human as much as is possible for one human to understand another. But empathy without theoretical grounding goes only so far. And theory, formulations, and assessments without empathy are fine for diagnostic purposes but standing alone make for a hollow therapeutic relationship.

I learned a lot about being a therapist during the years I myself was seeking professional help for my mysterious fear and anxieties. From these experiences I gained personal knowledge of what constitutes effective therapy.

My first attempt to get help took place when I was failing in adulthood, too nervous to teach or continue my graduate studies at the university. My family doctor referred me to a psychiatrist. I had no idea how the psychiatrist was going to help me. I just trusted he had skills and expertise that would somehow make me better.

I was in my twenties, married to Harvey, and living on the thirteenth floor of our bedbug-infested modern apartment with the great view. The psychiatrist listened compassionately and put his arm around me at the end of our first session. I melted. It felt so good. I really needed a compassionate guide. But soon he was interpreting my dreams as lesbian fantasies. What's more, he suggested I was turned on sexually by him. I couldn't believe my ears. I knew I felt nothing sexual for him. He was a skinny little guy whose trousers slid up to expose pale hairy legs. I was actually somewhat repulsed. As for his suggestion that I had sexual feelings for my childhood friend, Charron, who kept appearing in my dreams, I knew that was ridiculous.

The psychiatrist prescribed Valium for me. On the days I took it I felt buoyant and self-possessed. Fortunately I knew it was dangerous to solve my emotional difficulties with a pill. I used pharmaceutical relief very sparingly.

Eventually my psychiatrist moved his office from the anonymity of the Medical Arts Building to the hospital where Harvey was an intern. I couldn't face meeting Harvey's classmates when I went for my weekly appointment. I took advantage of his move to get myself out of his helping hands. What if I'd accepted his interpretations? Even then, although I still had no self, I knew he was wrong about me. He didn't get it. And of course he never got anywhere near the secret about child sexual abuse I kept even from myself.

My next therapist was Dr. Helen Morley. By this time I was established as a yoga teacher. Helen was a General Practice Psychotherapist. I chose her because Harvey didn't support my seeing a therapist; her services were covered by our insurance so I didn't need to find the money to pay her. Helen and I first met when she attended my yoga classes. She was training in bioenergetics. I pretended I was seeing her for the same reason she came to my yoga classes—to explore a new type of body consciousness.

Then came the day the insurance people mailed a routine letter to Harvey asking him to validate the number of visits I had made to Dr. Morley. Harvey was furious. I was misusing the insurance funds to pay for my entertainment, he said. I tried to explain I really needed Helen's help. "What disease do you have?" he wanted to know. If I needed therapy and he didn't know about it, our marriage was in worse shape than he'd thought. It was a stab in the back for him professionally. I was going to a kook while he was an acknowledged expert. I can't really blame him for not knowing how difficult everyday life was for me. I hid it well, even from him.

I managed to continue my work with Helen and she became a lifeline for me. It always surprised me that no matter how depressed I felt entering her waiting room, I always left her office feeling better. Looking back in my journals, I see that I repeatedly wrote, "Thank goodness for Helen," followed by the details of our session together. Here is a typical journal entry:

April 14, 1976
I'm surprised recently to realize how hard I've pushed myself to be something I'm not. There's no way I'd want to be any of the old Marys. But I have to avoid demanding too much of myself emotionally. I am really angry at times. And sometimes I am really irritable or afraid. Even though these states don't fit with my smiling, composed self-image, I have to admit I feel these things.

Helen asked me to describe the self image that these feelings could not be a part of. I thought of other people—yoga teachers for the most part—who were so controlled and serene that you couldn't get near them emotionally. I said I wanted to shake them and say, "Who are you?" I don't want to get stuck on being a plastic model. I just want to BE.

It was years later, when I recovered my memories of childhood sexual abuse, that I realized I needed further therapy. This is when I returned briefly to Helen and then settled in with Dr. Ralph Bierman. Ralph was the grand old man of Focusing-Oriented Psychotherapy who moved to Toronto and set up a private practice. He just listened, without trying to figure out whether my story was true. He gave no advice and had no agenda. His empathy and compassion gave me the courage and support to do whatever I needed to do. When it became clear to me I needed to disclose to my mother and sister, Ralph supported me fully.

He always seemed glad to see me when I arrived for my appointments. He tuned into my thoughts and feelings, validating and deepening my sense of myself. I became more who I was. His respect for me increased my own sense of self-respect. We came to care deeply for each other in a relationship of trust and mutual high regard.

From these three therapists I have distilled some qualities to look for in a good therapeutic match, no matter what type of therapy you choose.

Even though you are dealing with distressing issues, most days you should leave your session feeling lighter and more optimistic than when you arrived.

You should feel your therapist "gets you"—that you are understood and respected.

You should be assured the therapist understands the issues you are dealing with and has the skill and training to deal with those issues.

Chapter 18

Guidelines for Healing

This final chapter outlines some of the common problems faced by adults who have been abused or neglected as children. In it I offer information that has proved helpful to me and to my clients over the years. I talk about knowing whom you can trust, how to form a relationship that's safe, whether to forgive those who have betrayed you, the need for structure in your life, the importance of relaxation, exercise, and meditation, plus the importance of being successful in something, and, perhaps most important of all, the need to build a self.

Whom can you trust?

Survivors of childhood trauma tend to fall into two categories: those who trust everybody and those who trust nobody. Neither style represents true trust. When you think about it, it's no wonder trust is a big issue for people who were neglected or abused as children. When they were vulnerable and helpless, the very adults who were supposed to be looking after them betrayed them. Lacking models of trustworthy people they never learned who was safe to trust. To make matters worse, children who dissociate their abuse don't learn from the bad experience since they don't remember it. The next time their perpetrators violate them, they walk, unsuspecting, into the same traps—and then forget all over again that it ever happened.

What is real trust and how do you know somebody's trustworthy? This is important to learn. If you didn't learn it as a small child you can get the hang of it as an adult. To discover whether you can trust someone, you need to observe people over time. Some people can be trusted with your money but not with your confidences, and vice versa. Observing a person in many different situations gradually lets you know how he or she treats others. Is this a person who tells lies in order to get his way or cheats when she thinks she won't get caught? Does this person recognize and respect others' feelings? Does he or she remain loyal to friends? Check it out. Be an astute observer.

Perhaps it's safe to say that every human has some weakness or issue they struggle with. Once you know what it is, you're in a position to protect yourself from their flaw. Once you know, you may end up saying to yourself, "Oh, that's what it is. Well, that I can live with. I'd like to get to know that person better."

Relationships

Relationships are built in tiny steps. It's important to remind yourself that you don't really know somebody until you've spent time with them in many different circumstances. First impressions may be lasting but they are not necessarily correct.

Even though our hearts yearn for closeness and attachment, we need to proceed slowly. It's worth waiting for the right people.

The world is full of predatory, dishonest, manipulative types. It's your job to separate the selfish and uncaring from the decent people. When a good person joins you in a relationship, this is a precious gift. You need to pull them into the centre of your world. These trustworthy people with whom you feel respected and safe will provide a buffer between you and an often harsh, exploitative world.

There will be people in your life, however, from whom you will need to create distance. These are the people who leave you feeling less, who treat you with contempt or exploit you. Such people have to be pushed back far enough that they don't hurt you.

In the process of healing, you are the most important person. Anyone who gets in the way of your healing, even if it's family, has to be pushed into the background. Sometimes a complete parentectomy is required if abusive parents choose to maintain their illusion of a model family rather than help you recover. Such parents will never ask for forgiveness for their past abuse or their failure to protect you. In a case like this it may be necessary for you to "divorce" the family.

Forgiveness

Forgiveness requires that both parties participate. The wounded party discloses the past abuse. The other party must hear the charge and express remorse for the harm that was done. Without this there is no real forgiveness. Forgiveness is a two-way street.

Most important is letting go of the hurt and pain we carry inside us. It's hard on our health to carry anger and hurt. Whether you ever confront the adults who betrayed your trust is far less important than finding inner peace. Ultimately, in the process of healing your trauma, your organism will release the hurt and anger it has held. But this can be a long process, one in which the organism restores its original wholeness, free of what happened and what was done to you in the past. This is not something that can be rushed. Forgiveness, in the sense of no longer feeling hurt and angry, will come on its own when the body/mind is ready to truly let go of the wounding. What happened in the past will just not be very important.

Structure Versus Chaos

If your head is in a fog and your life has been buffeted by whatever forces pushed and pulled you, it's time to grab the reins of your own life. Take charge.

Start with a daily routine. Get up and go to bed at around the same time each day. Have a plan for the day. Even if you're not going out to work, plan an event or job to be accomplished.

Choose the day's priority. Whatever else, this one thing will get done. If you're the sort of person who procrastinates, your priority on a given day may be to get a certain job done, perhaps to make those neglected phone calls. On the other hand, if you manage your anxiety by keeping frantically busy, your priority may be to practise self-care by soaking in a warm bath for twenty minutes or listening to music. Rescuers, those survivors who put everyone else's wants ahead of their own, need to establish boundaries so they don't neglect themselves in their compulsion to fix others.

If you're finding it difficult to get out of the house or motivate yourself, choose a trip to the post office or a bit of grocery shopping as that day's event. Regularly take yourself just beyond your comfort level. That way you'll expand your tolerance for stressful events. Avoidance of life doesn't help except in the short term. You may feel a sense of relief at the time, but your world will become smaller and smaller until you're staying home most of the time or going to work and returning to the shelter of your home shutting out the riches of the world.

Relaxation

For some survivors deep relaxation is the hardest thing to do. If you find the relaxation at the end of a yoga class or the meditation you are learning brings an emotional flood of nameless fears, you are probably experiencing feelings related to unresolved traumas. In this case maybe you should wait until later in your healing to explore relaxation and meditation. In the meantime, it will be helpful for you to remember the fear you experience is the child's fear—the terror you felt as a child. There is almost nothing in your adult world that could scare you that much. You're more likely to be sad or angry about what was done to you back then.

For everyone else, learning to release the stress from your physical body and to quiet your mind will bring a sense of calm and comfort. You're going to benefit from mastering some relaxation techniques in order to handle the stress of therapy and the physical and mental tension of dealing with your childhood. Experiment with different relaxation CDs, join a relaxation class, or learn one of many approaches to systematically relaxing the body. Just knowing you're able to create an oasis of calm at will can make a big difference.

Learning breathing techniques can put you in charge of your emotional state. We cause ourselves to panic by hyperventilating. That means we can also alter our physical/emotional systems by breathing. Learn one of the many yoga breaths. *Pranayama* (yoga breathing) is the type I am familiar with and has many variations. But there are other types of breathing for you to explore. Choose the one that works for you.

Exercise

Many abuse survivors are completely out of touch with their bodies. They've always walked around numb to their physical selves. This makes sense. It's been scary and uncomfortable to feel their bodies' responses to life. To live fully, though, we need to be in touch with our inner knowing—and this means connecting with our physical selves, inhabiting our bodies.

Yoga, Tai Chi, or Pilates trains you to be mindful and in the present moment with your physical self. Group sports, running, jogging, walking, swimming—all of these and many more forms of exercise will release the tension in your muscles. Perhaps the most important criterion is that you enjoy whatever you choose to do.

For me, yoga and running formed the perfect combination. Running provided the cardiovascular fitness yoga lacks. Today I use yoga, low-impact workout classes, plus the treadmill or walking to keep my body healthy. And for you? Yoga may not be right but give it a try, along with a number of other approaches. Again, the important thing is to discover what appeals to you.

Mindfulness

Mindfulness—or the practice of being in the present moment—is the opposite of being dissociated. Learning to be mindful is vital to healing from trauma. Practise totally concentrating on brushing your teeth, preparing a meal, or watching a sunset.

You'll be rewarded with a sense of time stretching out and the world becoming still. There are many forms of mindfulness. Again, choose the one that is right for you.

Daily meditation (giving yourself this quality of attention each day) repairs early damage from lack of attachment and inadequate parenting. Now you are the one caring about and attuning to yourself. Meditation is empowering, improving one's connection with others as well as with one's self. There is scientific proof that meditation enhances the function of the prefrontal cortex, the part of our brain that determines our judgment, maturity, and empathy with others.

Success

Nothing helps poor self-esteem like success. Become good at something. Maybe your success will lie in writing poetry or creating crafts. Find out where your talents lie and what brings you pleasure. Get involved in these areas. Improve your tennis game or take up running. Running is especially empowering and uses up lots of fight-or-flight energy.

If you choose a sport that makes your heart pound and your breath come in gasps, you may experience this windedness as frightening. In the past, panting for breath and a racing heart were associated with fear. Keep telling yourself it's healthy to puff and pant when you're in charge and getting healthy.

Your healing is worthy of at least as much energy and attention as vocational training or a university degree. Unless you work on healing, nothing else shines brightly. Family, partners, children, professional success, all are experienced through the dull, gray fog of dissociation. And once you give to yourself the gift of peace and self-worth, everyone else in your world will benefit.

Build Yourself a Self

This whole book has been about how I built my self. I started out as a child who didn't dare express an opinion different from my mother's, who kept a low profile out of fear of worsening an already intolerable situation, and who spent much of her life fogged over to dull the inescapable pain of incest. I learned early that no one was going to help me and—in those days—that nobody would believe me. All I could do was rein myself in tight and avoid conflict.

Once I left home I sought out friends who were safe to be with. They were ethical people who cared about the world and their fellow humans. They were careful never to exploit or take advantage of others. This was the sort of world I wanted for myself. Over the years I learned to pull good people close to me wherever I found them.

Through yoga I came alive in my body. I also learned, eventually, that even the guru didn't know what was right for me. Becoming a yoga teacher gave me confidence and built my self-esteem. I was one of the people who helped make yoga the respected practice it is today. I feel really good about that.

Eventually I wanted my work to be accepted by mainstream society. I felt marginalized as a yoga teacher in the seventies when yoga was still considered a countercultural activity. That's when I applied to the School of Social Work to earn my master's degree. I'd set myself a difficult challenge. It had been seventeen years since I'd been to school. I succeeded after a great deal of hard work, thereby increasing my self-esteem. I proved to myself that I was not a "dumb bunny," the label I'd pinned on myself in my early school years. Graduation gave me the stamp of approval from the professional world.

I have been very fortunate in my choice of teachers. Swami Radha changed my life forever. When the time was ripe I found Dr. Eugene Gendlin as a teacher. It was from him that I learned to trust my own knowing. Dr. Ralph Bierman supported my growth and was a model of what a therapist could be. Through the many years he listened to me and kept me company on my journey.

There's no doubt about it: I built a self—an authentic self. Each of us needs to do the same, searching out the right path for ourselves and the right people to help us along the way.

Conclusion

Back in the Wonderful Years, when I was in my fifties, I had a dream. It was one of those dreams with a special quality, the kind you never forget. Here's how I described it in my dream journal, in April 1990.

> I am a singer standing alone on the stage of a huge concert hall. My voice soars, filling the hall with its richness. The sound seems to wrap around each person sitting there. A rich contralto rises up effortlessly from my belly.
>
> Then my song finishes and the crowd cheers, deeply moved by my voice. I step off the stage to join Harvey. Together he and I greet hundreds of audience members whom we recognize as survivors of childhood sexual abuse. My heart goes out to them as I hold their hands and encourage them to go on with their healing. Then come their friends and supporters, followed by helping professionals.

All of us are joined in the work of healing past traumas and in the fight to prevent child sexual abuse in the future.

My dream was clearly counter-factual. I can't even hold a tune. In hindsight I see that the dream looks forward to the time I would write *Confessions of a Trauma Therapist*. The emotion in the dream matches how I feel about my book and how I am sending it out into the world to help those who are suffering from child abuse and to help others to understand the shame, pain, and loss that result from childhood trauma. And above all, how it offers the hope that healing can be a journey out of darkness and into life.

LaVergne, TN USA
23 April 2010
180357LV00005B/2/P